The Material Culture of Zimbabwe

H. Ellert

Sam Gozo (Pvt) Ltd

Longman

Longman Zimbabwe (Pvt) Ltd/Sam Gozo (Pvt) Ltd
Tourle Road, Ardbennie, Harare

Associated companies, branches and representatives throughout the world

First published 1984

ISBN 0 582 61393 0

Printed by Mardon Printers (Private) Limited

Contents

Acknowledgements

Mrs S. Nduku (Ethnographer at the Harare Museum for permission to photograph and for general discussion); Mr Chris Till (Director of the National Gallery, Harare, for permission to photograph items); Mrs A. Kamba, Director of the National Archives of Zimbabwe (for photographs); The Ministry of Information, Posts and Telecommunications (for some photographic material); Mr Paddy Grey (who kindly took many of the photographs at the Museum and Gallery); Mr D. Huggins and Mr B. Chidyamatamba (National Arts Foundation for encouragement and some photographs); Mr A. Chigwedere, Ms C. Thorpe (Harare Museum); Sr E. V. de Oliveira (Museu de Etnolgia in Lisbon for showing me their collection of Mozambique and Angola); Mrs Pam Kriek and Ms Julia Gwindi for typing the manuscript; and great thanks are due to Marilyn Poole and Nda Dlodlo who both encouraged and guided me in this venture. Dr Ngwabi Bhebe read the first draft.

The author and publishers wish to thank and acknowledge the following sources of photographs and other illustrative materials:

1 Ministry of Information for photos on the following pages: introduction, 8, 27, 62, 65, 67, 75, 80, 91, 92, 97, 102, 111, 117, 123 and 126.
2 National Archives of Zimbabwe for photos on the following pages: 4, 5, 9, 15, 31, 35, 41, 50, 74, 79, 82, 87, 88, 120 and 127.
3 National Museum of Zimbabwe for photos on the following pages: 96, 98, 100, 101 and 110.
4 National Art Gallery of Zimbabwe for photos on the following pages: 19, 23, 24, 25, 26, 27, 28, 29, 30, 33, 34, 36, 38, 40, 42, 43, 46, 53, 54, 55, 56, 60, 64, 67, 68, 69, 70, 71, 76, 77, 78, 81, 86, 95, 96, 98, 99, 102, 103, 109, 112, 118, 119, 124 and cover.
5 Globe and Phoenix Gold Mining Company Limited on page 99.

Samuel Gwarega Gozo was born into a business family in Chibi on 14 April, 1936, went to Goromonzi in 1950 and the University of Rhodesia and Nyasaland in 1957. He graduated with a BSc in Chemistry and Zoology.
In 1960 he joined the NDP and became chairman of the Highfield Youth League. In 1962 he accepted a grant to study for a Master of Business Administration in Atlanta, Georgia.
He worked for American Metal Climax, Inc. in New York before joining the Rhodesia Selection Trust Ltd. in Zambia in 1964. In 1974 Gozo became materials manager for General Electric Company of Zambia. He became marketing manager for Mashonaland Holdings in 1977. He also had a spell with the Ministry of Industry and Trade (1979-1981) before going into business in mid-1981. He is now chairman of several companies in which he bought interests.
Married to Valencia, with three children, Unathi, Ropafadzo and Pedzisai, his hobbies are tennis and horse riding. "I am a lover of African Culture and during my extensive travels in Africa I have bought an enviable collection of makonde carvings from South Tanzania, wood masks from Zaire, mpani figurines from Zambia, metallic figures from Lagos and several paintings of the African way of life."

Author's note

A great debt of gratitude must go to the hundreds of ordinary people who willingly and hospitably received me into their homes to discuss and show me something of a rich cultural heritage. It is from such people that the inspiration to write this book came.

This account of Zimbabwe's material culture is certainly not complete but by including subject matter from various parts of the country, my intention has been to present a truly Zimbabwean picture. Any greater emphasis on one region or another or omissions of material should not be misconstrued as a deliberate attempt to present this or that culture as being better than any other, but rather as being best illustrative, in my humble opinion, of the material culture of Zimbabwe as a whole. I am well aware that there is still much to fully investigate and document. The subject is literally so vast and comprehensive and volumes could be written on most of the subjects covered in this book, not to mention aspects not touched upon such as clothing, bells and gongs, charms and traditional medicines, rock paintings, soapstone carvings and figurines, decorative walling and architectural styles, fire-making, tattooing, etc. This book is confined to the more tangible and material facets of Zimbabwe's culture, i.e. the artifacts of daily use in the past and present.

Hopefully this introduction will be accepted in the spirit that I intend — to communicate to a wider audience, both at home and abroad, a glimpse of the fascinating world of Zimbabwe's material culture and to extend to the more serious minded student a challenge to continue a job just begun.

Introduction

In pre-colonial Zimbabwe, technology and the arts were successfully combined to produce the material requirements of a culture dating back a millenium. Study of this interesting and highly fascinating aspect of our culture shows that the people of Zimbabwe had developed technology appropriate for the manufacture of tools, implements, weapons, vessels, musical instruments and ornaments of all kinds which demonstrate ingenuity and originality, a sophisticated understanding of the natural environment and above all, a quality of life in which cultural values were fully appreciated. They developed a fine sense of aesthetic understanding and splendid examples of this can still be found, albeit on a diminishing scale, in the pottery, musical instruments and other artifacts of daily life.

Archaeological evidence of the jewellery and pottery from early times right through to the nineteenth century is available, although much of this was destroyed around the turn of the century by the unscrupulous activity of men who worked for the Ancient Ruins Company of Rhodesia.

In the sixteenth and seventeenth centuries, Portuguese chroniclers like Fr Francisco de Monclaro, Fr João dos Santos and Diogo do Couto made some very useful written observations on the material culture of Shona people they encountered. In the nineteenth century, Karl Mauch, Thomas Baines and Theodore Bent made further contributions. Noted for their observations of Ndebele material culture are Thomas Morgan Thomas, the Rev. David Carnegie[1] and Dr Neville Jones.

The society and culture of which we speak has its roots in a history stretching back one thousand years to a time when a Shona speaking people settled on the plateau region of modern day Zimbabwe. Approximately two hundred years after their arrival, the early Shona raised up stone walled settlements which were to become symbolic of power and prestige. The most important of these is the Great Zimbabwe near Masvingo. The ruling or dominant class built huts within the stone enclosure whilst the bulk of the population established their homes beyond the walls. Pastoral and agricultural activities were the major occupations of these people.

1 Carnegie, David, Among the Matabele.

The Great Zimbabwe

The mining and smelting of iron, copper and gold also featured prominently. Ornaments and weaponry were wrought from these metals. It is likely that outlying rural populations of this Zimbabwe state might have paid taxes to the central ruling authority in the form of sorghum, cattle, goats, ivory and gold. The Great Zimbabwe administration might also have required its subjects to work on the improvement of the stone walls at Zimbabwe and other locations.

Inter continental trade was one of the most important activities of the Zimbabwe State which maintained such relations with sea borne traders through the coastal outpost of Manyikeni[2] in the Inhambane province of Mozambique. There is now some modern archaeological evidence that Manyikeni was an independent outlyer of the Zimbabwe State.

Some time around the early or mid fifteenth century Great Zimbabwe went into decline and a gradual dispersal of the population followed. Many of the citizens of Great Zimbabwe relocated themselves in the Zambezi valley and elsewhere on the high plateau region of Zimbabwe. Simultaneously, the Torwa state, already in existence at Khami, entered into a period of even greater prosperity and authority.

The break up of this State has been attributed to a number of reasons: the struggle for control of the coastal trade amongst rival factions, the inability of the environment to support such a massive urban concentration and the possible fall in the water level of the Sabi river which was the major route to the sea.[3]

It is not known for certain whether the Munhumutapa dynasty was already established by the time Great Zimbabwe declined but it is from this period onwards that the new state became better known. The Mutapa or Munhumutapa dynasty under its

2 João Morais and Paul Sinclair, Manyikeni, a Zimbabwe in Southern Mozambique. September, 1977, 8th Pan African Congress on Pre-History, p. 4.
Trabalhos de Arqueologia e Antopologia. No. 1, pp. 1-10, Maputo U.E.M. (for evidence of connection).

3 Historia da Africa, edicão do Dept de Trabalho ideólogico, Frelimo, Janeiro, 1978 p. 52.

founder Mutota established itself in the Zambezi valley somewhere in the Dande region. Their descendants are the vaKorekore people of N.E. Zimbabwe and the Tete province of Mozambique. The walled ruins of Zwongombe hill in the Mount Darwin district were probably the capital of this state for some time. Mutota was succeeded by Matope and during his reign he is said to have expanded the territory under his domain to include nearly all lands between the Zambezi and Sabi rivers. Animal husbandry, mining, agriculture and weaving of cloth and trade were the major activities of the people. (This expansion of the Mutapa State clearly accounts for the ethnic and cultural similarities still prevailing between the people of N.E. and the East of Zimbabwe and neighbouring regions of Mozambique.)

The power of the state weakened in the seventeenth century and the disintegration of the authority of the Mutapa occured around 1864-84. Because the seat of the Mutapa or Munhumutapa was located in the Zambezi valley, outlying population groups, especially those of the higher plateau of what is now Mashonaland, Manicaland and the adjoining provinces of Midlands and Masvingo, were more or less autonomous — although subject in varying degrees to the Changamire influence from around c. 1700.

Before this development was the existence of the isolated culture which thrived in the highlands of Inyanga until their dispersal and general assimilation sometime around the 18th and 19th centuries. The best examples of this culture are its system of hill terraces, stock pits and stone walled enclosures of which the Van Niekerk ruins near Inyanga are the best known.

Meanwhile in the west, the Changamire/Rozwi were dispersed by the invading impi of Gundwane in 1838, and Mzilikazi in 1839. Subsequent wars and gradual assimilation led to the formation of the modern Ndebele people with their own cultural traditions. For purposes of this book, these were combined with those of the rest of Zimbabwe.

Trade goods imported by the rulers of the Zimbabwe and other states included fine cloth (known as *machira)* of cotton, silks, porcelain, beads and other luxury items. These were exchanged for gold and ivory. During later centuries when trade was monopolised by the Portuguese who succeeded to the existing trade routes left behind by the Arabs, more consumer goods such as cloth *(machira)*, beads, brass and copper wire, porcelain, *ndoro* and other items were introduced and bartered for precious gold and ivory.

The Zimbabwean Archaeologist, Peter Garlake has emphasised that it was gold that brought foreigners to Zimbabwe throughout the last one thousand years. Arabs, Swahili and Portuguese traders brought their beads, textiles, ceramics and glassware to Great Zimbabwe to exchange for gold and ivory.

They also brought an even more incongruous and useless assortment of foreign baubles. None of this did anything for the economy. At best this trade was marginal to society, at worst it initiated exploitation which has lasted to the present day.[4]

4 P. Garlake, Great Zimbabwe, described and explained, 1982 Zimb. Pub. House p. 16.

During this Portuguese phase — lasting from 1500 to 1900 — a number of wholly indigenous industries were revived and took on greater importance for the communities in which they were practised. Cotton cultivation and weaving were introduced — as far as can be determined — by the Muslims at the same time that they introduced intercontinental trade. The production of *machira* (cotton cloth woven on low wooden looms) is thought to have been marginal to the overall economy before 1505 and the minimal rate of cloth imports afterwards might well have stimulated local *machira* production. The reliance on locally forged iron did suffer from the competition of imported material. This does not appear to have adversely affected the Njanja iron trade which flourished during this Portuguese era up until after 1890 when cheap hoes were imported and which marked the end of this important pre-colonial industry. The gradual decline of the local cloth and iron industry accelerated after the effective seizure and annexation of Zimbabwe in the 1890s by the administration of the British South Africa Co. which marked the beginning of the colonial era in Zimbabwe's history. The occupation forces slowly consolidated their grip over the country and after the first Chimurenga (or Chindunduma) of the late nineties, they started dismantling traditional authority and patterns of life. Indigenous cultural values were suppressed and through forced labour and urbanisation people were exposed to western influences alien to their own culture. The colonial mentality frustrated, degraded and strangled Zimbabwean culture and artistic traditions in their efforts to bring 'civilisation' to the 'natives'.[5] Thus the forces of competition from superior technology, urbanisation, forced labour on farms and mines and a different concept of artistic appreciation, all took their toll. The traditional industries and crafts that have survived, did so in a hostile climate in which much has been forgotten. This problem was identified during the revolutionary struggle and positive measures are now being taken to reverse this situation. (Hence the creation of the Culture division of the Ministry of Sport.) All this does not mean that the Zimbabwean national character was so suppressed during the colonial era that traditional cultural values were completely abandoned. Many cultural traditions were revived during the struggle against colonialism. Music and song were adapted to modern versions of the Mandarendare and Nyamaropa. Nationalist leaders popularised animal skin hats and carried symbolic walking sticks *tsvimbo* (Shona) *intonga* (Sindebele), as token of national identity and pride. The spirit medium institution by which family ancestors come back to help

5 J. B. Nyoka, Herald, 21.10.81. Article in Harare Herald, Zimbabwe.

their relatives in times of sickness or trouble also played a vital role in stimulating the Zimbabwean national character.

Despite such efforts it was perhaps inevitable that some change would come. The pressures of an alien culture were too great and time does not stand still. The younger generation, particularly those in the urban sector, is growing up ignorant of a vital aspect of their cultural heritage. The process of change and development into a new technological age is inescapable and necessary, but it is equally important to know and understand past traditions and their material culture. A better understanding of arts and technology, of how men and women strove to make the best of their natural environment may yet be of tremendous importance as Zimbabwe stands at the dawn of a new era of challenge and self determination.

It is against this background that we now review the ethnography of Zimbabwe, including the musical instruments, implements, tools, weapons, jewellery, textiles and other aspects which all combine to give us a better understanding of Zimbabwe's material culture, past and present.

1 Golden artifacts and ornaments

Destruction of a rich archaeological heritage

Perhaps unparalleled elsewhere in Africa, South of the Sahara, is the account of how a band of greedy adventurers destroyed a rich archaeological legacy by systematically tearing down the remains of ancient stone Zimbabwes in their quest for golden artifacts and jewellery. In the 1890s, African villagers were either coerced or bribed with gifts of blankets to reveal the location of these stone ruins and sacred burial grounds.

During September 1895, W.G. Neal, George Johnson, F. Leech and J. Campell brought into Bulawayo a consignment of ancient jewellery weighing some 5,2 kg. On 3 March 1896, they formed the Ancient Ruins Company[1] in whose name much of this destruction occurred. What means they employed to gather this hoard were not disclosed. Thereafter the Company proceeded to exploit all remains of ancient cultures to be found within the lands allocated to them by the British South Africa Company.

1 Ancient Ruins Co. Limited, letter from File RH 10/2/1 Neal to Johnson. See National Archives of Zimbabwe.

Following this initial haul of golden treasure some additional 42,5 kg were discovered consisting of necklaces, rings, tacks, nails, chains, beads and mountings for furniture beaten out of solid gold, the bulk of which was delivered into the possession of Cecil Rhodes who paid high prices for them.

Not content with tearing down walls, the Directors of the Ancient Ruins Company embarked on the exhumation of ancient burial mounds, stripping the skeletal remains of jewellery. In one grave alone they found as much as 2,7 kg weight of gold jewellery consisting of bangles on the legs and arms, necklaces and rings manufactured from pure gold. These grave robbers noticed that the custom seemed to be to ornament furniture with sheets of beaten gold nailed on with golden tacks. Corpses were found with what appeared to be wooden pillows *(mitsago)* overlaid with beaten sheet gold or leaf gold nailed on with pure gold tacks.

The Ancient Ruins Company was wound up in 1903, having become unacceptable to the Administration on account of criticism levelled at the planned destruction and removal of archaeological evidence. Rhodes, having been informed of its disgraceful activities — probably by Dr Hans Soner — took steps to terminate its charter. So, ironically enough, Rhodes himself contributed to the Company's eventual downfall.

However the damage had already been done, Zimbabwe's future generations were robbed of a priceless heritage, its many national treasures having been smelted down into gold bars and sold to the profit of men like Neal. In a letter written from the site of the Dhlodhlo ruins on the 23rd September, 1895, W. G. Neal made a number of wild and extravagant claims that his activities had yielded up vast quantities of golden beads, bangles, necklaces, wire and other fancy ornaments all amounting to a little over 5 kilos in weight. W. G. Neal said that in the following year, 1896, he intended to work at Great Zimbabwe where he believed he would get gold by the hundredweight.[2] In concluding his letter, to fellow company director George Johnson, he said that a consignment of golden curios had been taken to help boost the Company's shares.

A postscript to this despicable affair came in 1904 when a book was published in England entitled *The Ancient Ruins of Rhodesia* (Monomotapae Imperium) written by R. N. Hall and W. G. Neal. This book set out to document, in so-called scientific fashion, information on Ancient Ruins in Rhodesia allegedly explored by these two learned gentlemen. The truth of the matter is that the book was an attempt to cover up their own wretched activities which had now become an embarrassment to them. There is now good reason to believe that the Ancient Ruins Company did not find as much gold as they had hoped but the treasures they did find were smelted down and lost forever. The criminal damage they did to important archaeological sites in Zimbabwe is incalculable.

The behaviour of such men showed the lack of regard Europeans had for African culture and history. The idea that Africans possessed cultural values and a civilization independent of European culture was either inconceiveable or suppressed as a threat to their own plans. This attitude was later demonstrated in 1970 when the Rhodesian Front regime instructed that no official publications should state that Great Zimbabwe was without doubt an African creation.

It is against this background that we now examine the little that remains of this peaceful age and marvel at the splendid things created by the ancestors of modern Zimbabwe, a people considered by the colonialists to be savage, uncivilized and primitive. The places where many of these golden artifacts were manufactured include Great Zimbabwe itself (located near Masvingo), Khami (near Bulawayo), Dhlodhlo and Nalatale (near Shangani), Zwongombhwe Hill (near Mount Darwin — Fura Mountain), and a host of other lesser outposts of these main

2 Hundredweight, here used in a metaphoric sense, i.e. 1 hundred weight equals 112 lb or 50,4 kg.

centres. The destruction of golden artifacts says nothing of the damage done to fine examples of pre-colonial porcelain and pottery, little of which has survived intact. (See Zimbabwean pottery and ceramics.)

Gold mining technology

In 1514-15, Antonio Fernandes, the first known Portuguese to visit the high plateau of Zimbabwe, followed a route which roughly corresponds to the major gold producing regions of modern Zimbabwe. This gives a good indication of exactly how extensive this industry was.[3]

One of the earliest written records of gold mining techniques describes how

> 'they dig into the earth after the fashion of a mine and they go underground for the distance of a stone shot and as they go, they take from the veins the soil mixed with gold and gathering it they place it in a pot and boil it over a fire and after it has boiled, they set it aside and let it cool and once cooled there remains the soil and the gold and it is all fine gold . . .'[4]

Mining and smelting and manufacture of fine jewellery for the elite in society was practised in the Zimbabwe, Torwa and Munhumutapa States. Gold was drawn into wire as shown by the find of an iron instrument at the Dhlodhlo ruins with six gravitating holes of different gauges. Gold was made into tacks or nails and beaten into leaf used as covering for wooden stools, and pillows (*mitsago*). Gold wire was extensively used to decorate clubs, spears, wooden scabbard swords and other artifacts.[5] Following the arrival of the European and his demand for the precious metal, brass and copper wire quickly replaced gold.

Many pre-colonial gold workings can still be found in and around the major gold mining areas of Zimbabwe. The Globe and Phoenix Mine, once Zimbabwe's richest mine, is located on the site of one such working. Many other mines in the Kwekwe district have such ancient workings which all reveal a fairly sophisticated knowledge of mining methods including the use of supporting rock pillars and convection ventilation systems. The depth of these workings was normally determined by the water table. The excavations generally followed the reef where the ore was extracted by means of heating the rock with fire before rapid cooling with water cracked it. The ores were crushed in granite mortars many of which have been located in and around river systems close to the workings. Granite spheres, crucibles, iron *badza* blades, iron and copper bars have all been found during modern development from pre-colonial workings. Dishes for panning the gold in rivers were carved from wood or made from

3 W. A. Godlonton, Rhodesia Scientific Association Vol. XL April, 1945. Hugh Tracey, Antonio Fernandes, Rhodesiana, 1968 No. 19 pp. 1-26. R. W. Dickinson, Rhodesiana, 1971. R. W. Dickinson, Sofala, Gateway to the Gold of Monomotapa, Rhodesiana, 1968 pp. 33-46.

4 Diogo de Alcaçova., Documentos, Vol. 1 Cap. 47 pp. 389-391 (F. Barreto's expedition 1569-73) (Documents on the Portuguese). Francisco de Monclaro, Documentos, Vol. VIII Cap 26 pp. 325-429. The extent of gold mining is further confirmed in a narrative of Father Francisco de Monclaro during the expedition to Monomotapa led by Francisco Barreto around 1570 when he wrote . . . 'the interior abounds in more or less considerable mines, more or less being extracted depending upon their yield. They mine at certain times when they want to buy cloth to dress themselves with. They care much more for gold than we do, both for trade and for making the jewels and ornaments they wear. The Monomotapa gave some mines to sundry Portuguese who sojourned there, these, however, neglected them in favour of the cloth trade which is of greater profit, especially the "machiras" as was said.' . . . (F. de Monclaro, Documentos Vol. VIII, Cap. 26, pp. 325-429).

5 D. N. Beach, The Shona and Zimbabwe, Mambo, 1980, p. 106.

clay. In many cases, fig trees grow close to these early shafts which are often encountered filled with chipped granite. These chips have now become very characteristic of what are commonly termed ancient workings.[5a]

5a Interview with Mr B. Atkinson rtd., former Chief Executive of Globe and Phoenix Mine.

Jewellery and ornamentation

We have already seen how a great deal of the golden jewellery, removed from important monuments and archaelogical sites, was smelted down and sold to the commercial profit of early colonialist adventurers. When the Portuguese made contact with the Shona of Munhumutapa during the fifteenth and sixteenth

Shona smith and jeweller at work. He is pictured fitting arm and leg rings made from brass. Various other artifacts are also illustrated

centuries, they observed how women wore many copper rings on their arms and legs. Some of these armulets were also made of very fine golden threads or wire. There can be no doubt that the Shona people of that time had a fine appreciation of how to work in jewellery, for Portuguese chroniclers of the sixteenth and seventeenth century observed that the manufacture and wearing of golden jewels was common.[6]

6 Monclaro, Francisco de, Documents on the Portuguese. Cap. 26 Vol. VIII p. 429 (see also p. 381).

Ivory and hippo teeth provided yet another source of material from which ear lobe discs and other jewellery was fashioned.

One of the most lasting and popular forms of ornamentation for women were the armulets and leg rings. Made from imported brass or copper wire, they became symbolic of wealth and importance in the community. The brass or copper rings were known as *ndarira*, *tsambo* and *homo*. They vary in shape and design because this is determined by the jewellery smith and his sense of artistry. The other very popular and lasting jewellery form is the rich bead work which was often made from fragments of locally available snail shells or from the more expensive imported marine shells. (See Cowry shells.) The white calcium beads produced from this material were contrasted with black beads cut from ebony or some similar dark wood.

In the sixteenth century the Portuguese traded large quantities of beads made from clay, some green, some blue and some yellow. Traders carried these beads duly strung on *macuti* threads. These were known amongst the Shona as *miti* named after a measure of weight. These beads were exchanged with the Shona at Fairs or Feiras located at Luanhe, Bucuto and Masapa.[7]

7 Couto, Diogo do. Documents on the Portuguese Cap. 25 Vol. VIII p. 273.

Beadwork as jewellery

Combs

What has become popularly known as Afro combs were very common in pre-colonial Zimbabwe where they were often worn in the elaborate hairstyles. Some of these combs were fine examples of a traditional craft and served as useful toilet items and adornments.

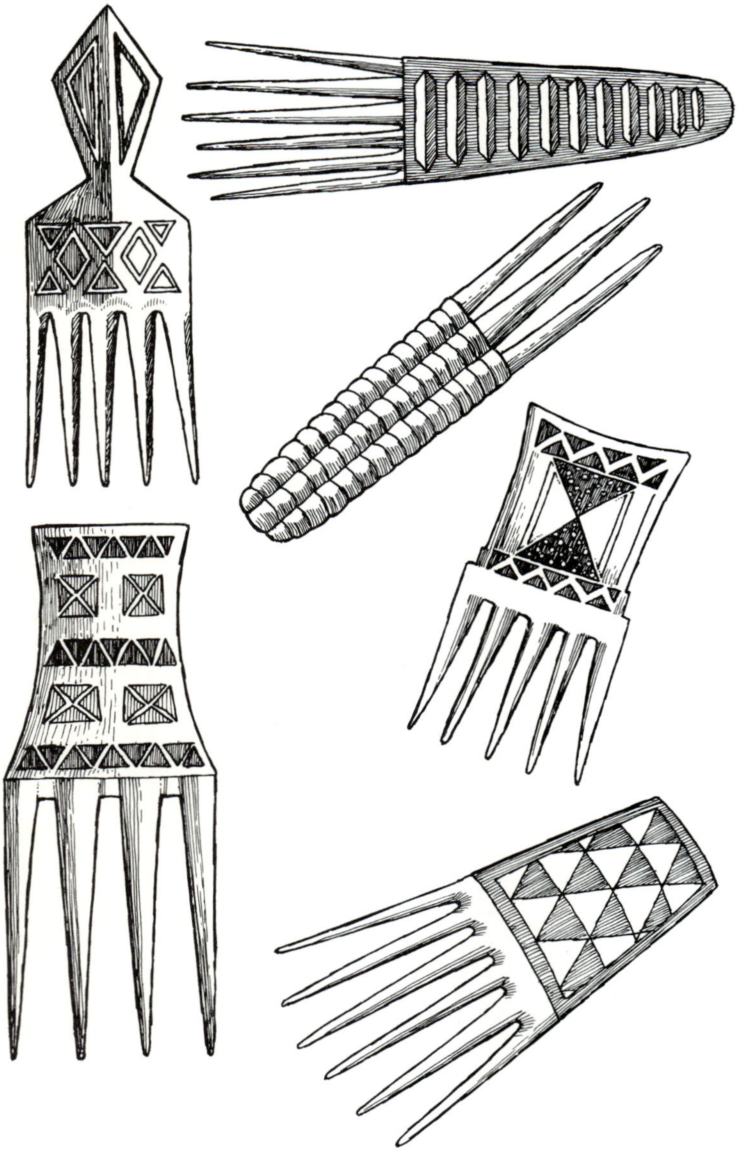

Carved wooden combs

2 Houses

1 Introduction

The material culture described in this book extends for approximately a thousand years. The architectural design of what is commonly known as the pole and *dhaka* hut has undergone little change over the centuries. Archaeological excavations at Great Zimbabwe and elsewhere reveal that the huts, up to 9 m across, had thick, low external walls built entirely of *dhaka*.[1] The surfaces were probably decorated with the widespread chevron patterns. The hut interiors were comprised of a clay built pot stand *(chikuva)*, the fireplace *(choto)*, seats and the sleeping platform. The grass thatch roof was supported by a framework of wooden poles which stood free of the walls. These poles might well have been carved or painted.[1a] The composition of a household was likely to have been exactly the same as it is today; consisting of the main sleeping hut *(imba yokurara)*, the kitchen hut *(imba yokubikira)*, together with the dormitory huts for young boys and girls respectively, the *gota* and *nhanga*.

1 Garlake P., Great Zimbabwe described and explained ZPH., 1982, p. 21.

1a Ibid

The houses of the rich or ruling class were enclosed by the great walls which were symbolic of the power and authority of those who lived within. Yet the houses of the common folk who lived beyond the walls were essentially the same.

In pre-colonial time, the highest concentration of people was probably that which existed in the valley area immediately below Great Zimbabwe. Most recent estimates vary from 5 000 to 11 000 people located in what amounted to high density urban living.[2] Lower concentrations did exist at Khami, Nalatale, Dhlodhlo and Zvongombgwe Hill, until those sites were finally abandoned, in favour of other locations.

2 Beach D. N., The Shona and Zimbabwe, Mambo, 1980, p. 46.

The Shona word *musha* has no direct translation in English and is used broadly to mean a family or clan grouping, or homesteads in the form of a village where everybody is closely related. This traditional closeness of *musha* has been greatly eroded by the pressures of time and foreign influence. In the western understanding of a family home, the various component rooms of the kitchen, bedroom and lounge are all joined together under one roof. The Shona concept of a homestead, in the traditional sense, comprises exactly the same amenities but as seperate integral units within a confirmed area or enclosure. In both cases the human needs are the same.

In rounding off this background to traditional housing in Zimbabwe it is interesting to note that the imposition of a special hut tax by the colonialist administration proved to be one of the major causes of the Shona risings of 1896-97 which marked the beginning of Shona resistance to colonial rule. The British South Africa Company had quickly realised that the African had to be forced into the European economic system. The Shona had shown great reluctance to enter this monetary system because

Village life

they were self sufficient, money had no value to them and they resented the intrusion of the whites. The tax was introduced and each hut levied ten shillings per annum. The administration calculated that the Shona would soon be forced to exchange their much needed manual labour in exchange for cash with which to meet the tax. The tax met with massive and unprecedented opposition, as witnessed during the Shona risings.

Ndebele military settlement

Huts again featured prominently during the Chimurenga war of 1972-1980. Over large areas of rural countryside, family homes were systematically destroyed and people were forced to live in so called Protected Villages (PVs)[3], where they would be unable to aid guerilla units. This policy proved disastrous and merely served to consolidate the resolve of the people to support the liberation forces.

3 The Man in the Middle. JPC publication, Salisbury, 1975 and Civil War in Rhodesia, C11R, London 1976.

2 The Shona homestead

2.1 Construction and components

In constructing a Shona hut, the first task is the roofing which consists of a conical shaped superstructure made from straight poles about 3 m in length. These rafters are lashed together with bark fibre and reinforced with interwoven lattice or wickerwork.

The circular shaped wall is the next stage in the completion of a Shona hut. The builder must mark out a radius and countersink a good number of upright poles around the circumference. These poles are reinforced by flexible sticks and tied together for extra strength. A mixture of cow dung and ant hill mud is prepared and thoroughly worked before being applied to the wall framework. A final plastering is applied to the interior and exterior after the initial application of *dhaka* has dried. In some regions, the external wall is not plastered. Among the Barwe of eastern Zimbabwe, hut walls are made from interwoven saplings which are unplastered. Grain bins are similarly constructed.

The westerly facing entrance way is fitted with wooden door panels hung on ox hide loops. The interior of the hut, in the case of the kitchen, still requires some additions. These take the shape of the elaborate pottery display shelf located on the opposite wall to the entrance way. The hearth is located centrally and clay benches built along the skirting inside the hut. The floor is also made from the same mixture.

The final task of thatching the hut now requires the attention of the men who carry out this important operation. Correct thatching will ensure that the roof is waterproof. Bundles of well combed straw are tied to the rafters starting at the bottom working towards the apex which is finally covered by a grass cap. Each lath is carefully secured to the rafters to ensure stability during violent thunderstorms and winds. A well prepared thatched roof can last for twenty years or more and many western style homes built during the colonial era adopted the thatch roof in favour of corrugated iron. The thatch is much cooler in hot weather and insulative during cold. The thatch is impermeable to water because the straw swells when wet effectively sealing the top layers from those below.

2.2 *Courtyard (chivanze)*

This generally consists of an area of cleared and well swept ground which surrounds all the houses of the family unit. What might appear to be stark and barren to western eyes serves many important purposes. This well swept ground affords an essential fire break from surrounding fields, permits early identification of night prowlers who might leave tracks. Snakes and rodents can easily be seen and despatched before they reach the safety of any hut.[4]

4 Du Toit F., Musha, The Shona Concept of Home, Z.E.D. October, 1981 p. 20.

2.3 *Kitchen hut (imba yekubikira)*

The kitchen is the heart of the home in all human society. Food is prepared and often consumed in the kitchen hut which is also the most important family gathering place. On entering a typical kitchen hut one comes across the clay pot shelf *(chikuva)* which is located opposite the doorway. The hearth *(choto)* is situated centrally and arranged with three stones on which the cooking pot stands. In recent times, a special metal frame supports pots on the boil. Raised clay benches are located around the edge of the hut providing seating. Often a small drying rack or basket *(mutariko)* is suspended over the fireplace in order to dry meat or vegetables. A whole range of household tools and implements are stored in the thatch and rafters of the kitchen hut. The smouldering wood smoke is said to contain preservative properties which protect the laths and the wooden roofing from decay and insect infestations.

In cooler climates, the fireplace is always within the kitchen hut but in hotter areas, the cooking is done immediately outside the hut. Within easy distance of the kitchen hut will be found a small wooden drying rack *(dara)* where pots and pans are left to dry in the sun, and a woodpile *(bakwa)*, providing fuel.[5]

5 Du Toit F., etc., p. 26.

The kitchen hut is perhaps the finest example of the traditional Zimbabwe house. It is the most elaborate in design and sturdiest in construction. Circular in shape, it has no windows in the western sense although ventilation is provided for by upward drafts which escape through the thatching or between the gap formed by the wall and the roofing beams. The kitchen hut can be used for alternative accommodation or to provide shelter for unexpected guests. In winter, the fireplace affords very welcome warmth.

2.4 *The meeting place (dare)*

Every homestead or village grouping has a central meeting place where important decisions affecting the family unit or the community as a whole are taken. Very often the *dare* is located under a spreading shade tree within easy distance of the homestead. Archaeologist have identified possible *dare* sites adjacent to Mazimbabwe (ruins of Great Zimbabwe and Khami era). Indeed the institution of *dare* convened during the difficult years of the liberation war (1972-80) as *Dare re-Chimurenga* or the supreme military council and Government-in-waiting. The Parliament of independent Zimbabwe is the ultimate extension of this concept now operating at a national level.

2.5 *Main sleeping hut (imba yekurara)*

The hut is located close to the kitchen and is normally unoccupied during the daytime. This dwelling is similar in construction to the kitchen although not equipped with the elaborate clay display shelf.

In recent times sleeping huts have taken on a rectangular shape in order to more readily accommodate beds and other pieces of furniture. Windows, too, are a recent trend towards better internal lighting and ventilation. Traditional sleeping mats are still more common than beds. Husband and wife sleep together in the main hut but in polygamous units the husband provides a separate hut for each wife and he himself has no fixed hut of his own, preferring to rotate.

2.6 *The granary (hozi)*

This extremely important building is a carefully constructed circular hut which is sub-divided into three or four internal storage chambers. The walls, floor and roof of these compartments are smeared with a mixture of cow dung and mud in order to afford maximum protection for the precious cereals and grains stored there. The hut is covered with the standard roofing which extends outwards in order to form something of a verandah which is often supported by a ring of poles. The granary hut floor is raised clear of the ground, by a full metre, and stands on supporting stone pillars. In cases where the granary is built on granite kopjes this is not necessary. By raising the granary some protection against rodent and insect infestation is provided and ventilation can take place.

2.7 *Dormitory huts (nhanga and gota)*

Similar in basic construction to all other huts these dormitories for boys and girls beyond the age of puberty are common features of most homesteads. Sexual awareness and the need for privacy is considered of great importance, hence the provision of these separate huts.

2.8 *Guest house (imba yavaeni)*

A separate hut will not be found in all Shona homesteads. More often than not visitors will sleep in the dormitories described above, which will be temporarily vacated.

2.9 *Livestock housing (danga)*

Sometimes known as the cattle kraal, this enclosure is found very close to the homestead for security. Similarly, a chicken coop *(zumbu)* is sited within the courtyard area. In pre-colonial days highly prized animals were kept inside the main sleeping hut in a special partition *(gora* or *huva)*, but this practice has now lapsed.

2.10 *Kitchen garden (bindu)*

Most homesteads will keep a small kitchen vegetable garden where pumpkins, cucumbers, green maize, cabbage, peri-peri and other vegetables are grown for domestic needs. The garden is generally located close to a water source or a specially dug well, and protected by a thorn bush fence to keep out goats and cattle.

2.11 *The standard hut and modern influences*

In some cases the traditional pole and *dhaka* under the conical wooden frame supporting grass thatching is giving way to more modern materials. Extensive deforestation and the availability of more durable materials are two reasons. The traditional circular hut is being replaced by rectangular brick-built houses fitted with windows and corrugated iron or asbestos roofing.

A typical rural homestead is so arranged that all the main huts face in a westerly direction. Here it is significant to note that the most decorative and impressive section of stone walling on the Mazimbabwe (Great Zimbabwe, Nalatale, Dhlodhlo, etc.) also face west. Any formal approach to a homestead is made from the west and as prevailing winds in Zimbabwe are mainly easterly, the kitchen hut is also located on the western side of the courtyard.

2.12 Decoration

There is evidence that in pre-colonial society houses were richly decorated by the carving of wooden beams and painting of the walls. Granary walls were often decorated with paintings of animals, birds and men. In other cases the interior of kitchen huts were decorated with black and white squares.[6] The nature of the external paintwork seems to depend very much on the artistic inclination of each household and decorative work is not a real feature of Shona society in the same manner as it is in Botswana and Southern Africa.

All huts were fitted with wooden doors and these were beautifully hand carved from selected timbers.[7] Very few of these elaborate door panels survive, but some can still be found in very remote regions of the country.

6 Bent,Theodore, Ruined Cities of Mashonaland. Reprint Books of Rhodesia, 1969 pp. 275 and 276. See also Garlake, P., Great Zimbabwe, etc.

7 Bent, Theodore, idem p. 259 (Hut Door).

3 A Ndebele homestead

3.1 Introduction

In the old military settlements of the Ndebele, huts were very much like the beehive style originally imported from Zululand. These huts had very low entrances which forced the occupants down on their hands and knees when entering or exiting.[8] The Ndebele later adopted the more sensible Shona style of hut construction with a larger doorway. Despite this adaptation, the Ndebele concept of a home is still distinctive in that most homesteads are surrounded by a fence of stout poles. The arrangement of the roof thatch reveals yet another difference.

8 H. Child, The History of the Amandebele, 1968 (Former Ministry of Internal Affairs) pp. 87, 88, 89 and 90.

3.2 Construction of a Ndebele hut

3.3 Roofing

Roofing poles measuring an average 2,745 m in length are arranged in a cone and tied together with fibres. Flexible osiers and wands are interwoven and tied to the superstructure creating a very strong and durable supporting framework on which the thatch is secured.[9]

9 Ministry of Internal Affairs

3.4 *Thatching*

Combed grass laths or bundles are arranged on the roof super-structure or rafters starting at the bottom working up to the top over which a grass crown is placed. In this manner the grass laths overlap each other forming a water-tight roof. The grass bundles are secured to the rafters by stitches and this work is done by two men. One man on the roof will pass the needle and fibre thread *(ugcamo)* through to the man inside in a standard sewing action until all the laths are well and truly secured, producing a beautiful layered effect.[10]

10 Ministry of Internal Affairs

3.5 *Walling*

A circular framework of poles (in some case reinforced by lattice or wickerwork of smaller saplings) is plastered with a well prepared mixture of cow dung and ant hill clay. In Ndebele society, decorations feature prominently, and red ochre is very popular as a colouring agent.

3.6 *Doorway*

The original Ndebele hut had a very low doorway which obliged occupants to scrape on their hands and knees. In later years they adopted the Shona doorway which extends the height of the walling. Door panels made from reeds were used by the Ndebele.

3.7 *Hut flooring*

The floor was prepared from the same mixture of ant hill mud and cow dung as used for walls, and was well stamped to form a durable cement-like surface. Vegetable juices, extracted in a mortar, are still used as floor polish.

4 Ndebele military settlements

4.1 *Introduction*

There were two main types of military villages, the first being a regimental village with an average population of between 500 and 1 000 and the second being the strictly military settlement housing *amajaha* (the young soldiers). The population of the military settlement averaged around 500.[11]

The villages were stockaded *(umdenga)* for defence and to keep

11 Summers and Pagden, The Warrior, Books of Africa, 1970 p. 24.

Huts

out marauding animals during hours of darkness. The villages were constructed on high ground within easy reach of wood and water.[12]

12 Ibid

In all cases the villages were built in a circular formation with each section of the huts similarly positioned towards the central enclosure where cattle were kept at night.

4.2 Granary (iziphala/izilulu)

Granaries or grain bins formed the outermost circle of huts adjacent to a stockade *(umdenga)* which was broken at intervals by special gates *(intshunguntshu)* giving access to the granary enclosure *(izibuya)* containing threshing floors *(iziza)* and grain baskets *(izilulu)*. These gates to the threshing area were secured at night. The grain bins consisted of a number of large baskets *(izilulu)* tightly bound together and erected on raised wooden platforms. The granary hut *(isiphala)* conformed more to the Shona style in that it consisted of a number of *dhaka* chambers within a hut constructed on stilts. The old Zulu concept of underground grain storage pits was finally abandoned during the 19th century. These pits worked extremely well as they were lined with ant hill and cow dung cement effectively proofing the chambers and precious contents for up to five years.[13]

13 Ibid

4.3 Kitchen hut (imikulu)

The kitchen huts formed the next circle of buildings. As with the Shona kitchen hut this building was also equipped with a raised clay display shelf on which pottery and basketware was stored. The hearth or fireplace *(iziko)* was located centrally.

4.4 Sleeping hut (izindlu)

The sleeping huts now formed the next ring and were inhabited by soldiers and their wives. Children generally slept in separate buildings located closer to the centre of the entire complex. These dormitories were known as *amaziba*.

4.5 Armoury hut (impalane)

Regimental shields were kept in a special hut — the *impalane* and these huts were located at convenient places next to sleeping huts. These special shield huts were much smaller than regular buildings.[14]

14 Ibid

4.6 Inner cattle enclosure (isilungu)

The cattle and other livestock were housed at the centre of the enclosure for security. In recent times the cattle kraal has been moved away from the main homesteads although some families still keep a special hut within the homestead area for calves *(isibaya samathole)*.

4.7 Outer stockade (utango)

The stockade was built from stout poles in the ground around the outside perimeter of the entire complex. More often than not it was reinforced by yet another fence of thorn scrub. A number of gates *(amasango)* were guarded at night.

5 Modern developments

The traditional Ndebele settlement no longer exists but the idea of an outer perimeter fence has been retained by many families. Doorways face to the west, away from the prevailing wind.

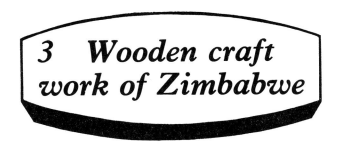

3 Wooden craft work of Zimbabwe

1 Introduction

Wood is an ideal material for the manufacture of a great range of artifacts. In most cases, only specific trees provided the type of material best suited to the use for which the article was intended. This chapter will examine many items, which were, and still are, in daily use throughout rural Zimbabwe. The production of these artifacts reveals how the natural environment was exploited to best advantage with a subtle combination of technological skill and artistic expression.

In making most of the wooden articles described in this chapter the craftsmen employ a variety of different sized shaping tools like the adze. Some large and others small, they are specifically designed for particular work — heavy and delicate. Thus spoons, bowls, pillows or headrests are made from the softer woods and axe handles and *duri* pestles fashioned from the heavier trees. This craft has, unfortunately, undergone some deterioration in recent years because of the availability of superior and more durable substitutes and the changing patterns of traditional life brought about by colonialism. (See appendix for a list of trees commonly used in the manufacture of many of the tools and implements described in this chapter.)

2 Wooden headrests or pillows

The wooden pillow or headrest, *mutsago* (Sh) and *umqamelo* or *umthiva* (N) occur throughout Zimbabwe and illustrates a highly developed form of artistic expression through the medium of wood. Although strictly utilitarian in its employment, the *mutsago* reflects considerable workmanship on the part of the craftsman. Perhaps it is indicative of the colonial mentality dominant in Zimbabwe until 1980 that little has been written on this highly creative art form. Perhaps they were regarded as nothing more than African artifacts not worthy of much serious attention. This is certainly not the case. Even a cursory glance will tell you that the craftsmanship reveals a sensitivity of mind and hand. Most examples collected are of an indeterminate age — perhaps from an era before the advent of western (cultural) influences — when such craft flourished in an atmosphere of free expression. Whatever the case, it is a fact that these artifacts are becoming increasingly rare as a general rule — an exception being the Nata area of Bulilimangwe where they are still widely used. Some modern headrests are being made but most of them fail to capture the detailed and intricate craftmanship of old.

In recognition of the artistic values symbolised by this artifact the National Art Gallery of Zimbabwe adopted a stylistic *mutsago* as their national emblem. The use of headrests by the nomadic people of the Sudan, Uganda, Kenya and Tanzania is common because they are both readily moveable and functional. Few of these headrests share the high standard of artistic merit of Zimbabwean examples. (See Headrests of Central Africa, p.21.)

In Zimbabwe, families possessing a *mutsago* look upon it as part and parcel of their cultural heritage and these have been handed down from father to son in strict lineal succession. Where the *mutsago* belonged to the spirit of a long deceased ancestor, it will be required during the ceremony preparatory to the appearance of that spirit.

During 1929, it was recorded that people of the Bikita region displayed a number of well fashioned wooden pillows. The pillows, made from the *mukombegwa* tree, were described as 'married people's pillows' because they were joined by a wooden chain. At the same exhibition, which was held in the former Victoria province (now Masvingo), an old black pillow made of finely polished *murwiti* wood was seen.

In 1932, further observations of the wooden pillows were made. They were reported to be in use amongst the vaKaranga who used them to preserve their elaborate hairstyles during sleep. The custom amongst the Karanga at that time was to allow the hair to grow quite long, tie it into curls well annointed with greases. During sleep these 'dreadlocks' were allowed to fall on either side of the head with a fillet keeping them in place. Pillows used for this purpose were elaborately carved and were much prized possessions.

The designs of the various *mutsago* do not appear to conform to any particular pattern and no significance can be detected in the absence of other evidence. However, it has been suggested that the two circular patterns common to some examples represent the female breasts but this cannot be substantiated. This would tend to suggest ownership or use by a woman whilst the other type of mutsago would have belonged to a man. As indicated by the general conformity of style and pattern occurring amongst the

Headrests in common usage during the 19th and early 20th century by the Shona

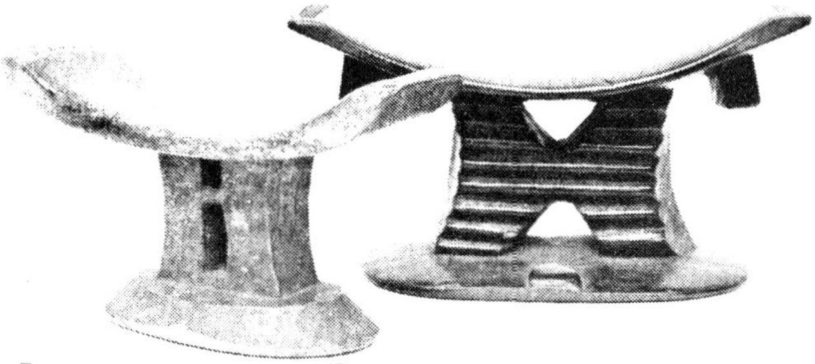

Example of headrests joined, carved from single piece of wood

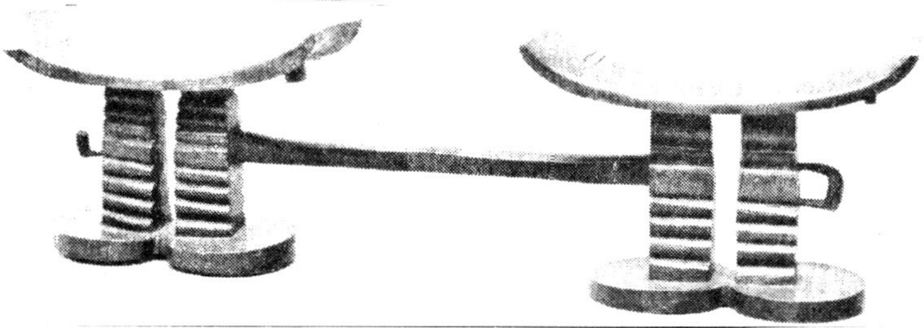

Headrests common in N.E. Zimbabwe

Headrest with vertical support pillar. Shows complete contrast of style

vaKorekore, vaManyika and the vaNdau, a more reasonable theory is that as a good design, it was much copied. The variations are likely to have taken place at the whim of the individual carver who after all was an artist susceptable to the foibles and inspirations common to all artists throughout the world.

Examples of *mutsago*, carved from a single piece of wood, as a pair for use by a husband and wife can be found and so can others linked together by a wooden chain. In such cases the *mutsago* is carved from a single piece of wood. Such pieces are splendid examples of the wood carvers' art. There is a colourful legend that the chains enabled one or other to warn his or her sleeping partner of the approach of danger by gently shaking the chain close to the sleeper's ear. Others have gone so far as to suggest that the chains might be symbolic of an earlier age when Arabic-Swahili slavers or their agents drew people into bondage.

In bygone days, men of seniority in the community, chiefs and elders, were expected to sleep with their heads raised from the floor. Such men often used elephant tusks as headrests. There does not appear to be any regulation regarding who could possess a *mutsago* although they might have been restricted to those who could either afford to buy one or carve it for themselves.

Mitsago measure on average 11 × 22 cm and an assessment of the age of some of the finer examples in our Museums and National Art Gallery is difficult. Some examples could be up to 200-300 years old having been conserved by the preservative properties in wood smoke within huts where they were generally kept in the rafters.

The use of *mitsago* in Zimbabwean society stretches back a very long time. It is quite likely that they were used by the people of the Zimbabwe and subsequent Torwa state of Khami whose wooden *mitsago* were covered with beaten gold nailed on with pure gold tacks. Such *mitsago* have been found buried with skeletal remains unearthed by the greedy gold seekers of the Ancient Ruins Company of Rhodesia operating in the 1890s.

During her sojourn through Zimbabwe in 1894, artist traveller Alice Balfour had this to say:

> '. . . nearly all these 'boys' carried pillows — small carved wooden stands with a concave top, on which to rest the back of the head. Personally, I would rather sleep with my head on the ground than resting on one of these, but tastes differ . . . The boys had earlier been duped by a certain Mr Coope who . . . accompanied us from Umtali (Mutare) and showed quite a genius in persuading the natives to sell their knives and other treasures. Mr Coope would begin by talking to them, gradually bringing them into such a state of good humour that they kept bursting into fits of laughter. Then he would proceed to barter for the article he wanted, and gradually wheeled them into pulling it out with reluctant hands and pathetic smiles, yet unable to resist the voice of the charmer and the bright rupees temptingly held before them . . .'[1]

These tempting rupees have not been altogether rejected as a Harare dealer in Zimbabwean artifacts often makes over two-hundred dollars on the sale of an antique *mutsago*. This

1 Alice Balfour, Twelve Hundred Miles in a Waggon, Reprint edition 1970 p. 214.

raises another issue and that concerns the preservation of national antiques within the country and argues against their export. In Arts Rhodesia of 1978, the artist writer Patricia Wood, on the subject of the *mutsago*, explained that a more poetic answer to the general use of the headrest came from a Shona himself, who said they were not for deep sleep, but rather for the gentle musings of the afternoon rest. Others said they were used only by the elderly.

Yet another observation on the use of the *mutsago* comes from Theodore Bent, who, in the early 1890s, noted 'they (the Africans) are utterly unaccustomed to postures of comfort, reclining at night-time on a grass mat on the hard ground, with their necks resting on a wooden pillow, curiously carved, they are accustomed to decorate their hair so fantastically with tufts ornamentally arranged and tied up with beads that they are afraid of destroying the effect, and hence these pillows.'[1a]

1a Bent, Theodore, Ruined Cities of Mash., Books of Rhod. 1969 p. 36.

Headrests of Central Africa

A particularly fine piece of craftmanship representing a carved wooden headrest depicting a seated male and female figure is located in the Kjersmeier collection of the Danish National Museum in Copenhagen. It stands some 19 cm high whereas most Zimbabwe headrests measure some 12 cm in height. The pillow stands on a beautifully carved rectangular base upon which two figures sit, a male and female with their arms resting on each others shoulders. The male figure, with a double tiered shoulder length head dress is on the left whilst the female on the right has an intricate cross shaped hair style. The faces reflect the typical Baluba (people who are distributed in S.E. Zaire and reputed to be some of the most skilful carvers in Central Africa) style.[2]

2 J. Nicolaisen and J. Yde, Art of Central Africa, 1972 p. 24 National Museum of Denmark, Copenhagen edition.

3 Divining instruments (hakata)

The use of *Hakata* was observed in the 16th century by a Portuguese named Antonio Caiado who was visiting the court of the Munhumutapa (Monomotapa):

> 'the ngangas (sic), the greatest sorcerers in the land, who forecast the future by means of four sticks — told him (the Monomotapa) that the priest (Silveira) had been sent by the Governor of India . . . to spy out the land.[3]

3 D. N. Beach, The Shona & Zimbabwe, Mambo Press, 1980 p. 93, Antonio Caiado to Luis Frois, Documentos Vol. VIII (15.12.1561) p.49.

Thus *hakata* (Sh) *amathambo* (N) were employed to determine the guilt of the Jesuit priest Fr. Gonçalo da Silveira in 1561. History has recorded that this impetuous man, who had made hundreds of impromptu Christian conversions on the coast at Sofala, was executed following denunciations of jealous Swahili traders and then cast into the Msengezi river in the Dande region.

The divining tablets can be made from bone, ivory or wood with bone being the most popular medium for their manufacture. *Hakata* is also the general Shona term for animal bones, *ndoro* fragments, fruit kernels and many other items which are all used by the *n'anga* and diviners to help in forecasting, and by herbalists to diagnose illnesses, and for various other uses.

The basic set of four tablets have specially designated values. Some authorities claim they represent *chirume* (the male) *kwami* (female) *nhokwara* (good luck) and the *chitokwadzima* (bad luck). Others maintain that they represent manhood or masculinity, motherhood, youthfulness and virginity or purity.

According to Ndebele cultural traditions, the person seeking a consultation must utter the phrase '*Ngizokhuleka*' meaning 'I have come for the bone throwing'. It will then be understood by the diviner that the visitor has come seeking advice or assistance from ancestoral spirits who will communicate such advice or warnings through the tablets. The art of being able accurately to interpret or read the tablets is inherited from an ancestor. A set of tablets will often be kept for several generations until a chosen descendent is nominated. He will then rightfully take custodianship/ownership of the tablets and will have the ability to interpret the meaning of the various combinations revealed after each throwing.[3a]

3a Interview Mr M. Ndhlovu. 7.11.82 Diviner.

Other items are sometimes required. These might be a special necklace, inherited from a forefather, together with the tablets. Such a necklace may consist of a combination of glass or ceramic beads interlaced with leg bones from an eagle and a vulture, the claw of a lion and a small piece of *gakamezi* (N) (tree root). This root has the positive effect of preventing the appearance of malevolent spirits which might prevent the successful interpretation of the bonesthrowing exercise.[3b]

3b Ibid

Hakata should be thrown onto animal skin or reed mat floor coverings. When not in use they may be kept in a special basket, woooden container or wrapped up in a piece of black cloth.

Although most often used as a set of four, the *hakata* tablets can also be employed in combinations of 8 and 16 with each piece inscribed with individual designs and meanings.

The *chitokwadzima* (bearing the crocodile emblem) appears as a bad or evil omen when revealed in combination with three blanks, i.e. the other three values showing the reverse face.

Should the *kwami* (bearing some 46 triangular shaped markings) be revealed in combination with the other three in reverse it would indicate yet another meaning. The possibilities are numerous and each throw has its meaning. The *nhokwara* tablet may have a total of thirty-five triangular markings whilst the *gata* may have about the same number.

Hakata in ivory

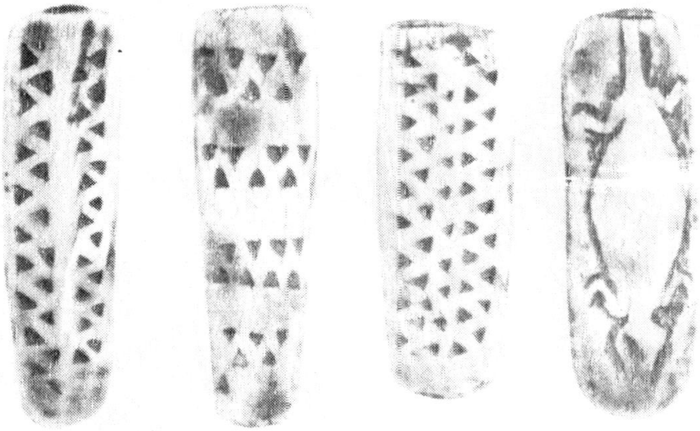

Hakata in wood

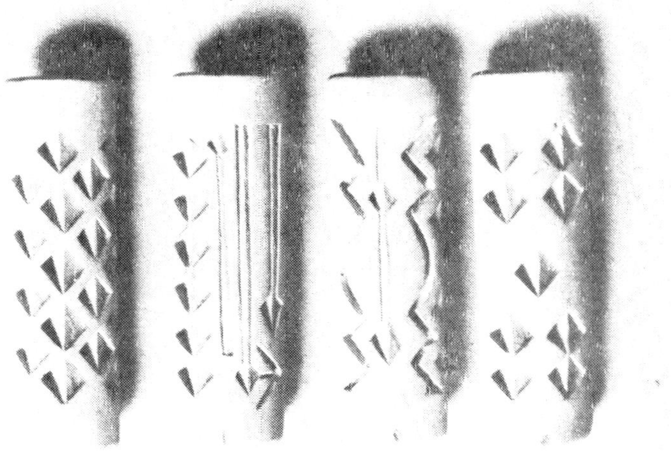

4 Phallic sheath (Umncwado)

Umncwado (penis protection device) was commonly used by Ndebele men who had reached maturity. Its use has almost totally disappeared since the introduction of European clothing. *Umncwado* was essentially used as a protection against irritation from flies. Whilst most of these phallic sheaths were made from wood, shaped into the required dimensions by the individual, they can also have been made from reeds linked together by tiny threads of *mupfuti* fibre. It was secured around the waist and worn under the skin or cloth apron covering worn back and front

— *amabetshu*. Youngsters were not permitted to wear *umncwado* and *amabetshu* was considered as sufficient protection until they reached maturity beyond the age of puberty.

Before wearing the device, it was sensible to sprinkle a good quantity of powdered *bande* wood into the sheath in order to prevent irritation or painful scratches from splinters in the wood.

The *umncwado* or penis protection device, carved in wood, was commonly used by Ndebele men. The phallic sheath was secured by means of a bark fibre string tied around the waist and worn under skin or cloth apron coverings. This particular example was found in the Nkayi communal lands

Umncwado

According to Ndebele traditionalists the main reason for wearing *Umncwado* was to cover the opening of the penis on the premise that this 'is the place where people come from'. It was completely taboo for anyone except a wife to see a man's uncovered penis. Without it, a man was considered completely naked — it mattered not that the rest of his genitals were exposed.

Umcwado was normally worn by securing it with string around the waist. It was important to secure it in this manner to avoid loss during exercise or fighting. If a man lost his *umcwado* during a dance, it was protocol to discreetly inform him, or request his wife to pick it up.

The secondary reason for wearing *umcwado* was for protection against injury in battle or to ward off ants when seated.

The wooden *umcwado* was considered far more durable and easier to clean that those made from ilala which often attracted lice and fleas. The wooden *umcwado* were sometimes made from the soft wood of the *uqoqoqo* tree which is common in Matabeleland.

The task of making *umcwado* was very specialised and left to a certain group of men in society. In order to 'size' *umcwado*, measurements of the young man's thumb and its circumference were judged to be equal to the length of the penis head which was all that required covering. Some sheaths were fitted with a small hole to allow seepage for those suffering from weak bladders — a condition known in Sindebele as *isicenene*.

Umncwado was considered a most important item and was regularly cleaned. When replacement was due a visit would be made to the specialists.

5 Wooden doors

The vaTonga people have developed a tradition of decoratively carved wood hut doors. Modern use of these carved panels is decreasing and fortunately some have been preserved in the collection of the National Art Gallery of Zimbabwe. Similarly, wooden doors are a feature of the Northern region of Mali Republic. Here wooden planks are carved with animal symbols. The hinge mechanism of the Mali doors are identical to that of the Zimbabwean door.[4] (See chapter on Zimbabwean houses for further details on hut doors.)

4 Art Zimbabwe National Art Foundation, 1982 p. 6.

Doors in common usage by the Shona during the 19th century

6 Stools

In most societies, a special seat is reserved for the head of the house and this certainly holds true in Zimbabwe. *Zvigaro* (*chigaro* for one) served a very practical function throughout the country. Styles differ from region to region with the commonest being the type carved from a circular piece of wood. The average height is 22 cm with a diameter of 30 cm. Generally, only men would sit on stools whilst women generally sit flat on the floor or squat on their knees. Within a family unit the father or head of the household has a special stool. Male visitors and household members will sit on the raised *dhaka* bench.

Selection of vaTonga stools

VaTonga stools

7 Staffs and sticks

5 Ambuya Nehanda, Ancestoral Spirit, manifested herself in a medium and led the 1896 Chindunduma Chimurenga before being captured and hanged. In 1972, Ambuya Nehanda again appeared and played a decisive role in the 1972-1980 Chimurenga.

6 A. Chigwedere, From Mutapa to Rhodes., Macmillan, 1980 p. 157 [30]

7 See Monclaro, Francisco de, Documents on the Portuguese Vol VIII Cap. 26 p. 379 (Simbo or Tsvimbo).

The spirit of Ambuya Nehanda[5] is said to have taken possession of a medium before crossing the Zambezi river into the region of Tete and N.E. Zimbabwe many centuries ago. On crossing the river, her medium reportedly struck the river with a wooden rod (*tsvimbo*) whereupon the waters parted and Nehanda and her followers crossed.[6]

In considering the *tsvimbo*[7] (Sh) or *umqwayi/intonga* (N) merely as a walking stick, one would fail to understand the importance of this item. For the ancestral *tsvimbo* plays an important role in the religious beliefs of the Shona people. In the illustration of the dancing medium, the *tsvimbo* would probably have belonged to an ancestor whose spirit (*mudzimu*) now possesses the chosen host. Family ancestors are able to give warnings and advice and generally assist in the well-being of his or her relatives. Thus this apparently simple artefact combining religious, artistic and practical qualities demonstrates the nature of Zimbabwe's culture.

A spirit medium dancing at the Chimombe ceremony. Clutched in his right hand is an ancestral *tsvimbo*

A selection of carved walking sticks

8 Plates, bowls and dishes

Wood is an ideal material for the manufacture of bowls, plates and dishes. Basins or pans for washing gold bearing sands have also been fashioned from wood. Some splendid divining bowls

Carved relish bowl from the Zambezi Valley Tonga people

have been carved out of wood and one particular example depicting a symbolic crocodile in the bottom of the vessel with signs of the zodiac around the rim was found near Great Zimbabwe.[8] The bowl takes the shape of a shallow dish richly ornamented with symbolic carvings. The divining bowl may well have been used by N'angas who were able to make predictions or interpretations according to the movement of small pips or corks which were allowed to float on the water. Similar divining bowls were also carved from soapstone.

A great variety of these vessels can still be found in daily use throughout Zimbabwe. More and more of the common *ndiro* (Sh) plates are being manufactured for sale in the urban areas. They are unpretentious in design and strictly practical. Some of the more richly ornamented and better hand carved plates and dishes, can, however, still be found in the countryside.

Dishes for cooked relish (vegetables or meat) and *sadza* tend to

8 R. N. Hall, P. W. G. Neal, The Ancient Ruins of Rhodesia, Methuen, (Reprint 1972. Books of Rhod.) p. 148. See also Bent, Theodore, Ruined Cities of Mashonaland, for wooden divining bowl.

Fine pair of wooden relish dishes carved in the Mutoko-Murewa region of Zimbabwe

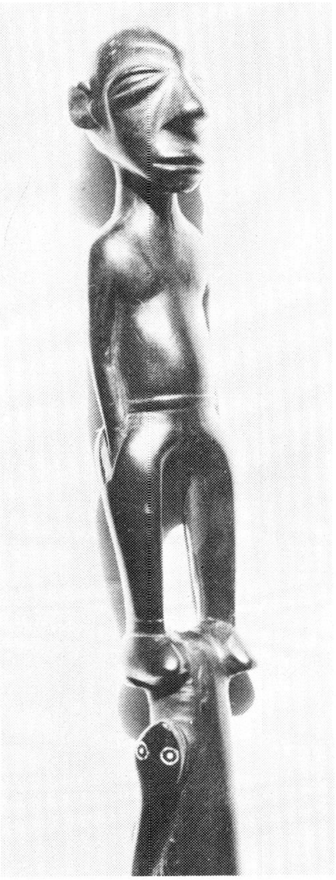

Carved walking stick from the 1960s. The man symbolises the European oppressor and the snake African nationalism rising to strike.

be better decorated than the plates. Whether or not a dish or plate is decorated with carving appears to be at the choice of the craftsman. There does not seem to be any set pattern in styles. Whilst dishes and plates are generally produced as single items they can be found joined together as a pair of relish dishes. In such cases, as with the twin headrests, they are carved from a single piece of wood.

The *ndiro* (Sh) *umganu* (N) plates are best carved from *marula* (Sclerocarya caffra), a white coloured soft wood and also from *mukwa* (Pterocarpus angolensis), a much harder darker wood for the more durable type of plate or vessel.

9 Spoons and ladles

Sadza is the staple diet of Zimbabweans and virtually every household throughout the country will have a *mugoti* (Sh), a sadza stirring stick in the kitchen. Because of the relatively heavy work of stirring the stiff sadza porridge, it is important that the *mugoti* is made from a strong piece of wood. Some of the best are made from the durable *umangwe-omkulu* (N) *(Terminalia mollis)* tree, with the black and yellow textured grain. This type of wood does not fray or splinter. Once the *sadza* is well-cooked, the *migwaku* (Sh) ladles are used to ladle the prepared food into serving dishes. There are two types of *migwaku:* the largest are for spooning *sadza* whilst the smaller is used to serve meat or some other relish such as spinach.

In strict traditional order, the thin *sadza* porridge is first mixed with the aid of the *musika* (Sh) whisk, then the heavier porridge

Sadza stirring spoons

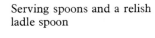

Serving spoons and a relish ladle spoon

must be stirred with the *mugoti* (Sh) and then ladled into the serving dish with the *mugwaku* (Sh) before being given a nice and smooth round appearance before serving. For this final stage, the *chibhako* (Sh) flat smoothing spoon, is used.

The water or beer ladle *pfuko yemikombe* is very useful for ladling water or beer as required. The ladle can be made of wood or simply from a suitably shaped calabash.

10 Mortar *duri* (Sh) *umgigo* (N)

The *duri* is found throughout the country and is indispensable for grinding maize meal and preparing foods like *dovi* (peanut butter). Smaller *maturi* are used for grinding tobacco for snuff and powdering of piri piri as a spice. The averge *duri* is 100 cm long and is made from the *mutiti* or lucky-bean tree *(Erythriana abyssinica) mubvamaropa* or *mukwa* *(Pterocarpus angolensis)* and *muriranyenze* *(Albizia antunesiana)* all of which are highly suitable woods, being durable and resistant to termites. Incidentally, most of these woods are also used in the manufacture of drums, wooden toys and other household implements.

In other parts of the country *maturi* are made from the *mutsamvi* wood *(Ficus burkei)* and the *mukute* or water-berry tree *(Syzgium guineense)* which grows in vleis. The wood of the *mukute* is strong and easy to work. It is also used to make dug-out canoes.

Whilst the *duri* is made from a softer wood, the pestle *mutsi* is cut from very hard wood such as the *mukonono* tree, one of the hardest known in the plateau country.

Maize meal being prepared in the traditional manner. Soaked maize seeds are first pounded in the *duri* in order to remove the outer skins. The kernels are once again ground in the mortar before being winnowed in the *rusero* basket. The final grinding process is undertaken on the *guyo*. According to traditionalists, maize meal prepared this way tastes best

Whilst most *maturi* follow the same basic shape, some are decorated with a carved band around the bottom section. This carved section may also follow a chevron pattern. Being an item of important and daily household use, there does not appear to have been such time for creative design.

A very early reference to the *duri* or mortar is found in Francisco de Monclaro's narrative on the expedition of Barreto to Munhumutapa in 1569-1573 when the Jesuit priest noted that 'the universal food of Kaffraria consists of porridge of lightly ground millet, or millet husked by means of pestles, which are large crushers'.

Another type of mortar is a very large tree trunk with mortar hollows made for the same purpose as those above. The corn was ground using the standard pestle. Teams of women used to pound the seeds in tandem. In some villages a small mortar, *isiganu* (N) is used as a container when milking cattle. Here the mortar serves as a vessel and has a particularly deep trough to it. In other regions of Nkayi, *umgigo* is used to grind medicinal herbs and also to prepare mash from the ground water-melon leaves which is used to polish and stain hut floors. This polish gives the floors a green colour and cement-like smoothness.

11 Cattle yokes

As much of Zimbabwe is still under peasant agriculture where the ox provides the power for the plough, the wooden *majoki* is essential for harnessing these oxen. Yoked cattle can be seen pulling two-wheeled carts providing a simple and cheap means of transport between villages.

12 Snuff boxes

Nowadays, snuff is usually carried in a tin. Older snuff boxes or containers are an unique art form. These were sometimes made from wood reeds or animal horn. They were decorated with geometric patterns and also with brass or copper wire work. Most snuff containers were made from specially selected gourds, spherical but tapering to a narrow neck which was plugged with a wooden stopper. Fine examples of these snuff containers can still be found in the Zimbabwean countryside and they often show the great ingenuity of the craftsmen.[9]

Similar containers, of a wooden tube fitted with a lid attached to the container by a leather thong, were used to store fats and grease. The grease containers were decorated with the brass and copper wire work common to much of Zimbabwean craft.

9 Bent, Theodore, Ruined Cities of Mashonaland, 1969 pp. 71-72.

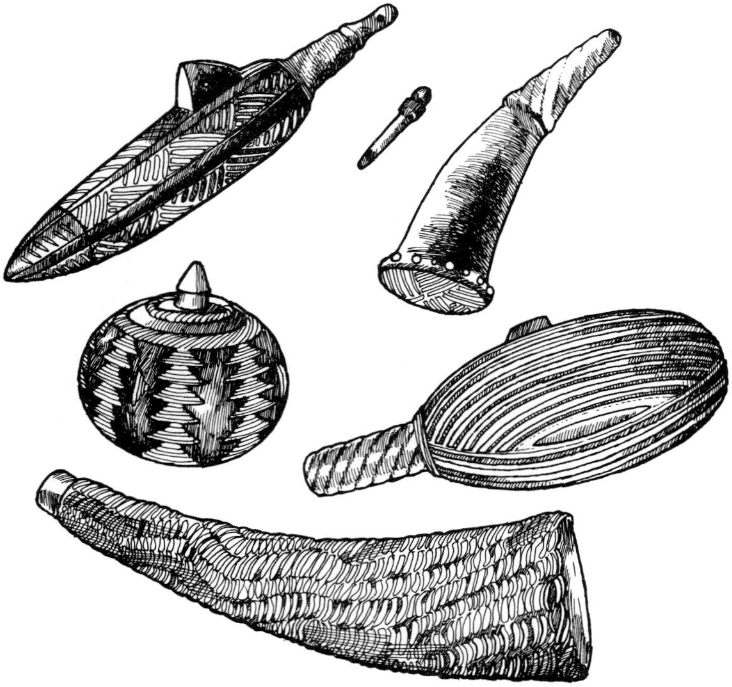

Snuff containers

13 Wooden trowels and scrapers

The flat bottomed wooden trowel *chikuvaro* (Sh) is used to smooth the mud and cow dung mixture applied to hut floors. This mixture is given a very smooth finish and after drying, sets as hard as cement. A polish made from ground vegetable leaves may well be applied to give the floor a green finish, similar to a commercial verandah polish. The wooden scraper — *humo* (Sh) is used to remove bark for the manufacture of the *gudza* (Sh) cloths. Because the scrapers are wooden, the bark can be removed gently. A steel cutting edge would be too sharp for this.

14 Cow bells

Evocative of rural Zimbabwe is the sound of the cow bells clanking as the cattle graze. Most cow bells are made from iron but the pair in the illustration are wooden and are from Manicaland. They produce a distinctive sound quite different from the iron bells.

Wooden cow bells

15 Dug-out canoes

Although dug-out canoes may well have served as a means of water borne transportation on the Sabi and other major tributaries of the Zambezi and Limpopo, it was along the former two rivers that they proved their real worth for people settled along their banks. Certainly the valley Tonga perfected the manufacture and use of canoes and so did the vaKorekore and the Sena of Mozambique.

During the years of the liberation war (1972-80), dug-out canoes were effectively used by villagers resident along the Zambezi to transport men and supplies. In order to effectively neutralise this system of river crossing, soldiers of the Rhodesian Government undertook the destruction of all canoes found along the Zambezi system from Victoria Falls to Cabora Bassa on the east.

This policy of destruction did not prevent the continued manufacture of canoes and since independence, many new boats have been built and are in daily use for fishing along the Zambezi. Today, the most effective use of these vessels is being made by the Zambezi valley Tonga for navigating the waters of Lake Kariba.

Canoes are often made from the *Munhondo* (Sh) (*Julbernadia globiflora)* but perhaps the best wood for the construction of canoes is considered to be the *mukwa* tree *(Pterocarpus angolensis)*. This valuable timber is one of the few woods considered best for making canoe paddles.[10] Its durability and special qualities also make it an ideal timber for dishes, mortars, drums and fishing spear handles.[11]

10 D. and C. Palgrave, Common trees of the highveld, Longman, 1973, pp. 43, 60.

11 D. and C. Palgave.

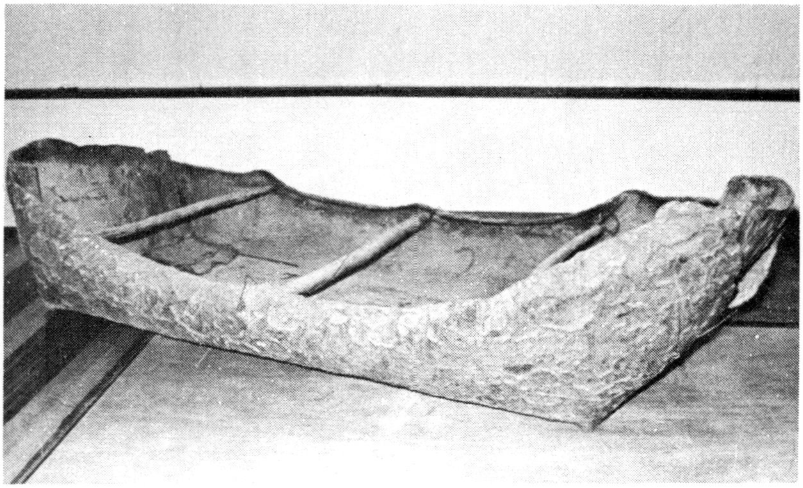

Dug-out canoe

4 Weapons and tools

1 Bow and arrow

In a sixteenth century campaign against the armies of the Munhumutapa, Field Marshall Vasco Fernandes Homem was seriously wounded when an arrow struck his right shoulder, pierced his thick leather jerkin and emerged the other side of his body.[1] The bow and arrow was an important weapon for the warriors of Munhumutapa, and Portuguese writers of that time tell us of its use against the invading Portuguese of the 16th and 17th centuries.

1 Diogo do Couto, Documents on the Portuguese Vol. VIII p. 293.

The technology for the manufacture of this type of weapon has existed in Zimbabwe since the stone and iron ages. The bow and arrow in Zimbabwe declined in the face of modern firearms and by the mid-1940s it had virtually disappeared from popular usage. In some remote parts of the country such as the Zambezi valley and the S.E. Masvingo province, it can still be found being used by rural hunters.

Bow and arrow

1.1 The bow (uta or wuta)

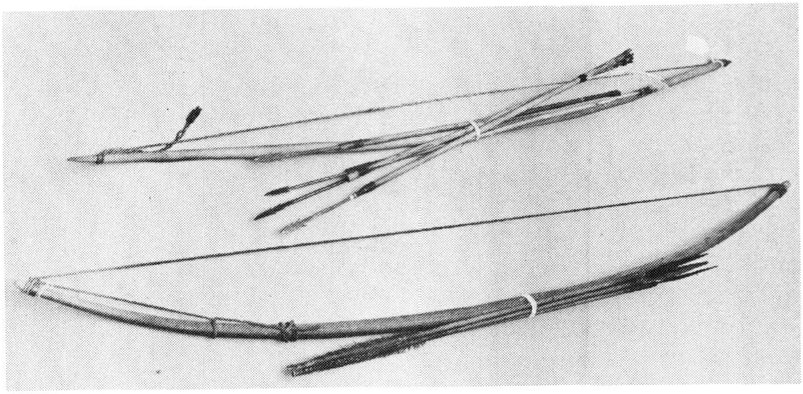

Bow and arrows

The bow was generally 2 m in length and cut from the *mutarara, mateswa, chiruwari* or *mutobgwe* trees. The length selected must be free from the knots and of a fine even grain.

Another popular wood came from the *mutongotowa* (dombeya rotundifolia) or wild peat tree common on the plateau country. Whilst the *uta* was the most popular, large all purpose bow, there were two smaller versions called the *dati* and *mukutu*. The dati was approximately 1 m in length and generally used by children to hunt birds and small rodents. The *mukutu*[2] was a medium sized bow.

2 Snowden, A.E. Some technological notes on weapons and implements used in Mashonaland, Nada, No. 17, 1940 p. 62 and Odendaal P. J. Nada. No. 8, 1930 p. 59 Bow and Arrow.

1.2 The bow string (rukungiso, rukusha, musungo or mukosi)

The bow string normally consisted of a strip of hide cut from cattle or wild antelope skin. This was made into a roughly semi-circular section, twisted and then suspended from a tree with a heavy stone. When perfectly dry the string was given a finish by rasping it into a true circular section.

1.3 Iron arrow heads (musewe)

Iron arrow-heads were locally smelted by craftsmen who traded them. Wooden arrow heads *(wamhina)* were occasionally employed when iron was unobtainable.

Prepared arrow heads of various types suited to particular needs were fitted to a shaft made of reed or wood *(rushanga, tsanga,* or *muteswa)*. These shafts were of varying lengths, weights and thickness. A barbed arrow-head designed to lodge firmly was called *musewe wenzeve,* the metal stem of the arrow head was the *runje,* the arrow point the *muromo* or *kumuromo,* the arrow blade the *chipanga* or *chipasa,* the central ridge of the blade the *musana* or *mudandara,* the shaft end the *nangiro* and the flight feathers *manhenga*. These flight feathers were taken from larger birds such as the *hungwe* or eagle.[2]

1.4 The arrow shaft

The arrow shaft was of varying lengths — between 30 cm and 50 cm. The arrow head was secured to the shaft with the aid of sinew *(runda)* bound tightly around the tip and smeared with a gum preparation of tree roots. Barbed arrow heads *(munyangowe)* were often smeared with a poisonous extract of the *uturu* bush (Strophantius Speciosus) which can be found in various parts of the country — but most commonly around Ndanga, Zaka and Chimanimani areas. These barbs were then carefully protected by wrapping them until required. Although poisonous to the wounded animal, the meat of game killed in this manner was not necessarily rendered inedible on that account as long as the affected area was cut away before being prepared for cooking. Arrows were stored in a quiver *(homwe yemisewe* or *mukutu)* until required. A fully charged quiver of arrows was described as *goga*. Quivers were not generally used but when required were made from strips of bark wrapped over a framework of thin osiers bound together with tree bark like *mupfuti*. Thus they resembled a deep basket. Other quivers were made from the hide of animals and these appear to have been more durable and practical than the tree bark type.

2 Axes

A varied and most interesting array of axes can be found throughout Zimbabwe. Many fine examples clearly show the combination of art and technology.

2.1 Tsomho

The *tsomho* or dancing axe is still very popular at religious ceremonies particularly among the Korekore where it is brandished by women whilst dancing. The *tsomho* has a slender handle and the axe blade itself is proportionately much smaller than of the larger *gano*. An interesting feature of the *tsomho* is the extension of the axe blade through the head or toe of the handle *(garo)* where it narrows and curves.

2.2 Humbwa – gano

Much more substantial in both weight of the blade and wooden handle is the *humbwa* or *gano*. This weapon was much used for defence and in hunting. The hunting of elephants by men armed with the *gano* is vividly reported upon by early Portuguese chroniclers, one of whom noted that:

'. . . two hundred men gather together with some iron tools

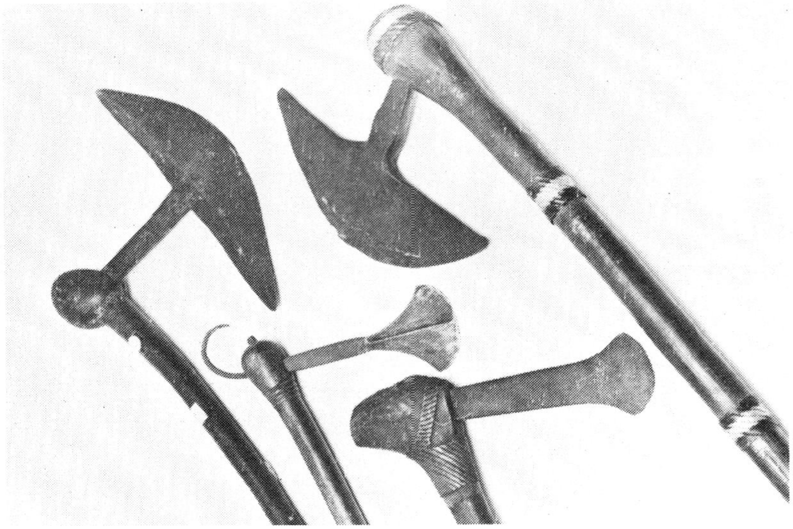

Hand axes: *gano tsomo* and *humbwa*

like hatchets and go to the place where they know the elephants come to pasture and they wait for them, and, when many elephants come together, the men give a shout that frightens the elephants and scatters them into the bush with the men after them and, as the bush is very thick, the big elephants get entangled in it and cannot turn.

The men come up and set about them with their hatchets hitting their hind legs (tendons) which are very tender, and in this way strike to the bone which, free of the flesh, cannot hold so large an engine and breaks and the elephants fall to the ground'.[3]

The *gano* or battle axe can be divided into two separate types, the first is the large semi-circular bladed weapon *(ruwe)* where the axe head is attached to the handle *(manyenza)* as pictured in the illustrations. The central metal stem is often decorated with cross hatching and other designs during manufacture. Of this type, some are more sturdy than others according to the intended purpose. *Gano* used for elephant hunting is very strong and durable and looks practical and effective.

The second type of *gano* appears to be more symbolic or decorative. Whatever the case, many of these weapons are extremely fine pieces of craftmanship. The *gano* handle *(manyenza)* is made from carefully selected fine grain dark or black wood. They are well balanced and often decorated with brass or copper wire. Centuries ago this would have been gold wire. The blades were often inscribed with cross hatching combining with the rest to produce a truly splendid work of art. *Gano* of this type generally measure some 50 cm in length with the steel blade some 8 cm to 20 cm from point to point.

Examples of the fine old *gano* are becoming increasingly rare

3 Br Baltazar to Fr Marcos, Documentos, 16.11.1560 Vol. VII see also Prendered A., Elephant Hunting. Nada, No. 8 1930. pp. 46-47 for contemporary account identical to the sixteenth century.

and it is truly a joy to hold and examine such a piece. Although modern versions can be found in popular markets or *msikas* they lack the artistic merit of the older *gano*, being designed for a mass market. Most often the axe blade has been cut from sheet steel whereas the genuine article was carefully fashioned by a village smith practising an ancient craft. Somewhat different in design is another type of *gano* or *humbwa* which features the axe head set into a large toe at the end of the handle. These axes resemble the more utilitarian *demo* and are generally used for clearing away scrub or chopping up freshly killed meat. These axes also reveal a high degree of craftmanship in design and manufacture and were often decorated with copper or brass wire work around the shaft.

The large semi-circular bladed *gano* is normally carried slung across the right shoulder of the man while he walks in an area where he might meet trouble. Otherwise the weapon will be slung across the opposite shoulder — of course depending upon whether he is left or right handed.

Decorations found on the *Gano* or *Humbwa* axes

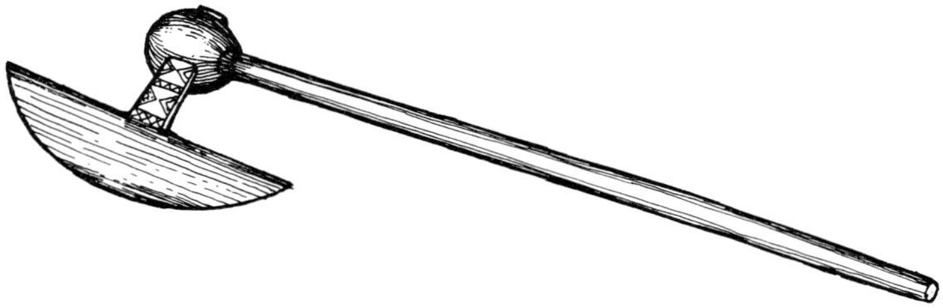

A very fine example of art and craft combined in the *gano* was described in 1949 when such a weapon, belonging to an elderly man, was examined:

> 'The haft of some glossy dark wood, probably pahla, and was held covered by decorations of wire, in chevron patterns alternating red and yellow. The blade was in the shape of a half moon, with a very narrow support. On the blade were numerous scrolls and vague patterns, scratched into the metal, conveying no meaning to the unpractised eye. This axe was a most perfect piece of craftmanship.'[4]

4 Hemans, T. J. Nyamkungedati and his weapon, Nada No. 26 1949, p. 66.

2.3 Ndebele battle axes

The Ndebele axe *(imbemba)* was introduced to them by the Shona. In an illustration from 1895, some Ndebele warriors are shown holding this weapon but early recorded evidence from traditionalists denied they were ever used in the old days. They are not mentioned in accounts of the *inxwala* and even description of the weapon identifies it closely with Shona culture.

2.4 *Demo*

Hand axe

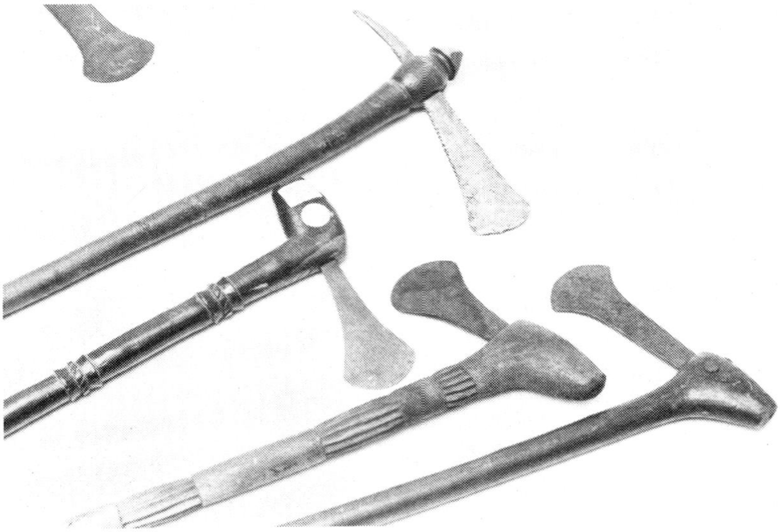

The general purpose *Demo* has many applications ranging from the chopping of firewood *(huni),* felling of large trees from which roofing, drums *(ngoma),* mortars *(duri)* and other items will be made. The demo was also used to fell large trees with a Y-shaped branch formation suitable for the sleighs *(chireyi)* which provided transport for heavy loads pulled by oxen. These sleighs were in common usage until officially discouraged because the continual dragging created water run-offs which quickly developed into dongas and contributed towards erosion. The *demo* consists of a large triangular blade *(ruwe)* which is set into the axe handle *(mupini)* which is often made from the *munondo* (Burkea Africana) or *matamba* (Strychnos Cocculoides) which are both pliable and tough. The *demo* blade *(ruwe)* might measure between 15 cm to 20 cm in length by 6 cm wide. A smaller version of the *demo* is called the *rutso*. In Matabeleland it is called the *ihloka*.

3 The adze or herminette

This general purpose tool *(mbezo)* is used in the manufacture of such implements as the *duri, ngoma* and *ndiro*. The *mbezo* used throughout the country is the carpenter's universal tool. The handle of this tool can be made from *mtamba* and in Shona is called *chisorokadzi*. Writing in 1894, Alice Balfour (artist and traveller) observed how men were engaged in the carving of wooden bowls by delicately hacking small chips off the outside of the bowl with a small adze, the blade of which was about 4 inches

Craftsmen busy with *mbezo* or adze

long and the cutting edge about 1 inch wide. The craftsman she observed had several of these tools with the blades set into the handles at various angles. One had the edges curved in at the sides. Another carver was hollowing out a bowl, which he firmly grasped between his feet while he scraped out thin shavings of wood with a small iron loop with cutting edges on both sides, fixed into the end of a wooden stick.

Quite apart from its use as a tool, the *mbezo* was once used in the Choka or Zoka rituals, practised in the 16th century. In this ritual a red hot adze was to be licked by a person accused of witchcraft, theft or adultery.[5]

5 D. N. Beach, The Shona and Zimbabwe, Mambo Press, 1980 p. 93.

4 The hoe

The hoe blade *(badza)* has a long tradition in agriculture and as a symbol of wealth. It was the single most important farming tool and whilst original versions have virtually disappeared, modern mass produced hoes are in daily use among the peasant farmers of rural Zimbabwe. From the name *badza* sprang the name for plough — literally *badza* or *mombe*. The *badza* blade as pictured in the illustration served an important role in marriage transactions. The *roora* was charged in terms of '*mapadza*'. It was also used as a digging tool in pre-colonial gold mines and many have been unearthed during modern development of such workings.

The basic *badza* comprises a large oval blade tapering to a point which is set into a wooden handle.

Three examples of Mhangura hoes

Hoe showing more modern influences in its construction and shape

4.1 Rupadza

A smaller version of this known as the *rupadza* or *serima* was fixed into a curved wooden handle. This gave the blade an inward slice and served to help lift clods of earth. The work was finished with the regular *badza*. The *rupadza* and *badza* blades, made of iron, would normally last up to five years with careful use.

5 Scabbard knives or daggers

5.1 Bakatwa

Bakatwa is the general Shona word for the wooden scabbard daggers which can be found in Zimbabwe. Although the concept of a scabbard dagger might well have been copied from coastal Arab traders who ventured into the interior many centuries ago, the particular type of dagger or knife found here has developed as uniquely Zimbabwean. The wooden scabbard *(hara)* comprises two separate pieces of wood bound together by brass or copper wire. The top section of the scabbard is usually richly decorated with intricate carvings of varying designs. The rear section of the scabbard features a wooden belt loop to allow the wearer to strap the weapon about his waist.

One of the earliest written descriptions of a weapon which appears to correspond to the *bakatwa* (short sword or dagger) can be found in the narrative of the expedition to Munhumutapa led by Francisco Baretto in about 1573. Francisco de Monclaro writing about the ill fated expedition commented that the warriors of the Munhumutapa used bows and arrows and some assegais. 'Most of them carry small swords of two spans length hanging from the waist with wooden scabbards. They also carry a *simbo*, which is a short club with a bludgeon shaped end, and which was the last weapon they throw in battle.'[6]

6 Monclaro, Francisco de, Documentos. Cap 26 p. 379 Vol. VIII.

In a record of enquiry commanded by Francisco Barreto, relating to the custom of the Munhumutapa and Manicas, Antonio Carneiro, in 1573 recorded of the Manica (Manyika) warriors that their weapons were bows and arrows, assegais and small swords *(bakatwa)* of perhaps a span and a half more or less. Similarly, the Portuguese historian Diogo do Couto describes how certain weapons were used by the warriors of the

Bakatwa, carved and ornamental swords

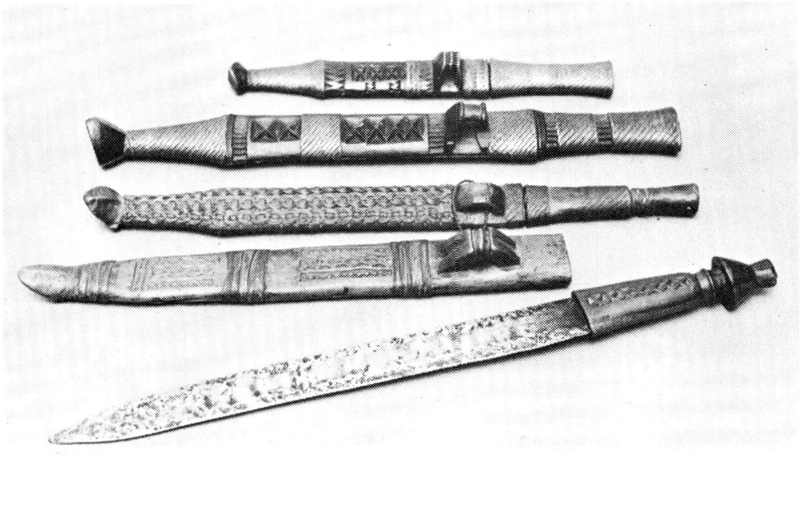

Munhumutapa in a battle against Barreto who led an expedition around 1573 - and mentions specifically swords.[7]

Alice Balfour during her travels through Zimbabwe in the 1890s observed how men carried knives, often with handles and sheaths most artistically decorated in patterns with fine brass or copper wire. She also described knobkerries and assegais being similarly ornamented.[8]

In the early sixteenth century the important men of the Munhumutapa society

> 'wore short swords in gold ornamented wooden sheaths, hung by belts of dyed cloth from the waist, and it is probable that these swords were carried by the Mutapa's chief war leaders.'[9]

The use of gold in ornamentation was common until the arrival of the Portuguese. In examining fine examples of *bakatwa* intricately carved and decorated with brass wire work it is easy to imagine how magnificent these weapons would have been with gold wire instead — the glimmer of the precious metal highlighting the rich grain and texture of the wooden scabbard. Such a *bakatwa* would be a great treasure and it is possible that a few such examples exist hidden away as family heirlooms.

The iron blade of the *bakatwa (banga* or *chese)* was beaten out from a central ridge so that one cutting edge was set slightly higher than the opposite edge. The blade was set into a wooden handle *(mubato).* The illustrations show a variety of *bakatwa* swords or daggers and the extent of the carved decorations and wirework on them. A smaller and simpler version of the *bakatwa* is the *banga* or simple sheath knife. This comprises a single edge blade secured in a double sided wooden scabbard virtually identical to the large *bakatwa* but without the fine wood carving. *Bakatwa* measure an average 43 cm to 100 cm.

7 Couto, Diogo do, Documentos. Cap 25 pp. 249-323 Vol. VIII.

8 Balfour, Alice, Twelve Hundred Miles in a Waggon, reprint, Books of Rhodesia 1970 p. 215.

9 Beach, D. N. The Shona and Zimbabwe, Mambo Press 1980 p. 106.

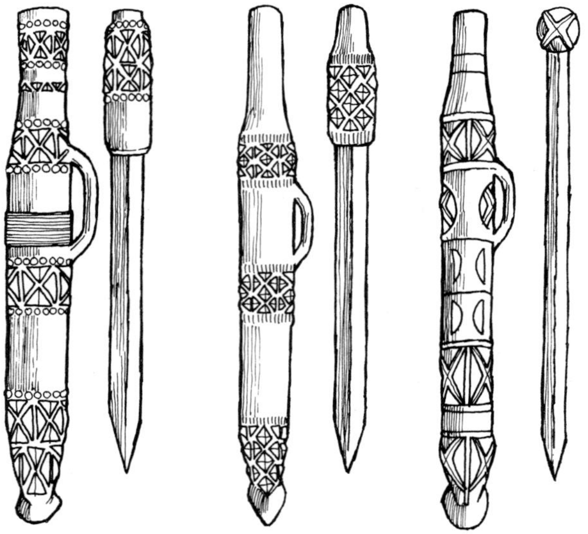

Bakatwa

The *Bakatwa* (large knife or sword) drawings show details of the blade *(chese)*, the wooden sheath *(hara)* and handle *(mbato)* all suitably decorated with interwoven brass or copper wirework. The average *bakatwa* measures 50 mm over length with a blade of some 30 mm x 5mm.[10]

In 1949 a District Commissioner of the colonial Native Affairs Department, stationed in Bulawayo, found a *bakatwa* in the possession of an elderly man journeying to Hwange. He described the weapon thus . . .

> 'the knife was into two parts, the blade was very sharp, made of iron, of native manufacture with no decorations of any kind. The handle was large and of complicated design, beautifully bound almost the entire length with yellow and red copper wire *(wukambo)*. The sheath *(nakara)* was made of two polished sections of a handsome dark brown wood *(pahla)* bound together with countless strands of the same wire. . . . The *bakatwa* and his other weapons, the old man explained, had been made by his great-grandfather. They had been handed down from father to son, and would when he died be handed to his eldest son.'
>
> An offer to buy them on the part of the Native Commissioner was spurned by the old man.[11]

10 Snowden, A. E. Some Tech. Notes etc., Nada 17. 1940.

11 Hemans, T. J. Nyamkungedati, nada 26, 1949 pp. 66-67.

5.2 Ndebele daggers

Contemporary versions of the *bakatwa,* without the carving and copper or brass wire ornamentation, are being made by Ndebele craftsmen. The best wooden scabbards are made from the *umangwe-omkulu* (N) tree (Terminalia mollis) which has a heavy black and yellow texture. The same wood is used to make sadza stirring sticks *(migoti)*. Traditionally, the dagger was not used by the Ndebele as the *isika* spear blade cut well enough.

6 The spear. Types of spears

The spears found in Zimbabwe can be divided into two categories, those used for hunting and those designed for warfare. The short stabbing spear or assegai was imported to Zimbabwe during the early 19th century when Mzilikazi and Gundwane trekked north from Natal. The long shafted and heavy bladed hunting spear of the Shona and the multi-barbed fishing spear of the Valley Tonga were already well established prior to the arrival of the Nguni.

6.1 The spear in Ndebele society

The spear *(umkhonto)* and the shield *(ihawu)* became symbolic of the militant character of the Ndebele nation of the nineteenth

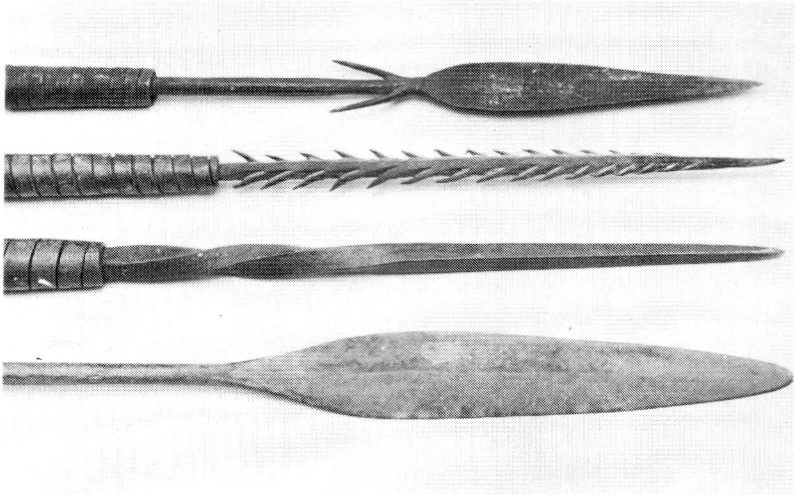

Spears illustrated show influences of Zambezi Valley. Tonga fishing spears and Ndebele stabbing assegai

century. There is a suggestion that the colloquial term Matabele stems from the seTswana word for shield, '*tebe*', and as this was the most conspicuous part of the Ndebele soldier's equipment, the name stuck.[12]

12 Jones, Dr Neville, Mhlangazanhlansi, My Friend Kumalo, Books of Rhodesia, 1972 p. 56.

6.2 *Ndebele military society*

In order to examine the great importance of the spear in Ndebele society, it is useful to look at the historical background of the people. Today, *impi* and *indlamu* dances, performed by the Ndebele, holding symbolic shields and spears, clearly evoke military traditions which date back to the 18th century and the origins of the Ndebele people. The Ndebele are descended from the Nguni, a Bantu people who still live in Zululand, Natal. In 1800, an expedition under a Zulu chief named Shochangane left Natal and finally settled in Southern Mozambique where his people were to become the modern day Shanganis. Gungunyana who fought against Portuguese colonialism around the turn of the century was a direct descendent of Shochangane. Later in the nineteenth century, Mzilikazi (1792-1868) moved north across the Limpopo river to join Gundwane who had arrived a year before. Together they dominated the Rozwi (around Khami) to become the founders of the modern day Ndebele people. Another Nguni clan under Zwangendaba Kumalo (1792-1845) also left Natal to settle in north-western Tete province of Mozambique and Malaŵi.

All of these breakaway families or clans took with them military techniques and cultural traditions which have remained to this day. The military equipment of a Zulu, Swazi, Shangani or Ndebele soldier of the 19th century was very much the same. A soldier of the Imbizo regiment *(ibutho)* in the nineteenth century wore a head-dress of clipped ostrich feathers *(indlukula)*, a cap of black ostrich feathers *(isigula)*, a leather apron or breech cloth *(ibhetshu)* sometimes superimposed by a kilt of monkey skins and wild cats' tails *(umtika)*, armlets of cow tails or ox hair worn about the elbows *(izigetsho)*; and finally, garters of skin worn below the knee *(imdloli)*.

To complete his military equipment, the soldier carried a large shield and a number of spears and possibly a knobkerrie as well. The shield served to identify his particular regiment and rank.

Still mindful of their heritage, many Ndebele men carefully preserve ceremonial headdress, skin, aprons, spears and shields which will be produced to mark special festivals of the Ndebele calendar such as *Umdlalo we zangoma*, *Inxwala* and *Ukuchinsa*. Certainly in the case of Ndebele herbalists and soothsayers the entire kit will be worn in formal dispensing or consultation. In most cases such clothing and weaponry has followed a strict line of inheritance and has strong connections with ancestoral spirits who speak through their chosen descendant.

The *Ixwala* or Great ceremony of the Ndebele people was presided over by Mzilikazi on one occasion during the mid-nineteenth century. At a particular moment of his choosing, he appeared dressed in a cap of otter skin with a long blue crane feather on his head, a cape of ostrich feathers *(isigula)* on his shoulders, a girdle of blue monkey skins around his loins and ringlets of long ox hair as garters and amulets. In his hands he held a huge spear and a beautiful shield of black ox-hide with one white spot. His appearance was greeted with great acclamation. The ceremony ended after the king had thrown his spear in the direction he had determined that raiding parties should venture forth. Young soldiers immediately rushed out to thrust their spears into the ground in a demonstration of support for their king.[13]

13 Ibid

In traditional Ndebele military society, all spears belonged to the King and all young men gave military service until around the age of thirty when they were permitted to take a wife. On the death of a soldier, his weapons would be returned to the royal armoury. Spears were issued to soldiers on graduation from military training when the young warrior became known as *ijaha*.[14]

14 Summers R. and Pagden C.W. Books of Africa 1970, p. 22.

In the early part of the nineteenth century, most of the spears used by the Ndebele belonged to the *isika* type which was still the same as the original pattern brought from Natal. This was the official or king's spear but early in the time of Lobengula's reign, the throwing spear *(isishula)* became accepted into the official armoury. This spear closely resembled the Shona (Karanga) hunting weapon and was most likely borrowed from the Shona. Similarly, various other spear types started to creep into the official armoury as Ndebele society became influenced by its neighbours.[15]

15 Ibid

By the late nineteenth century very few of the original *isika* spears remained. Most had been broken during combat and were either used as daggers or remade into new spear blade shapes which showed a variety of new shapes and designs copied from the Shona and the Zambezi Valley Tonga. Following the suppression of the Ndebele risings of 1896, large numbers of assegais were confiscated by the colonial authorities and examination of these weapons revealed over 15 different types[16] of blade showing considerable transformation from the original *isika* or kings spear. A number of European-made spear blades also found their way into Matabeleland during the nineteenth century — these were made by the English firm of Marples Brothers.[17]

16 Sykes, Frank W., With Plummer in Matabeleland, Books of Rhodesia, 1972 pp. 159-237.

17 Ibid p.136 (see description of Spears).

6.3 *Official Ndebele spears (imikonto)*

The official spears of the Ndebele can be divided into three main types:

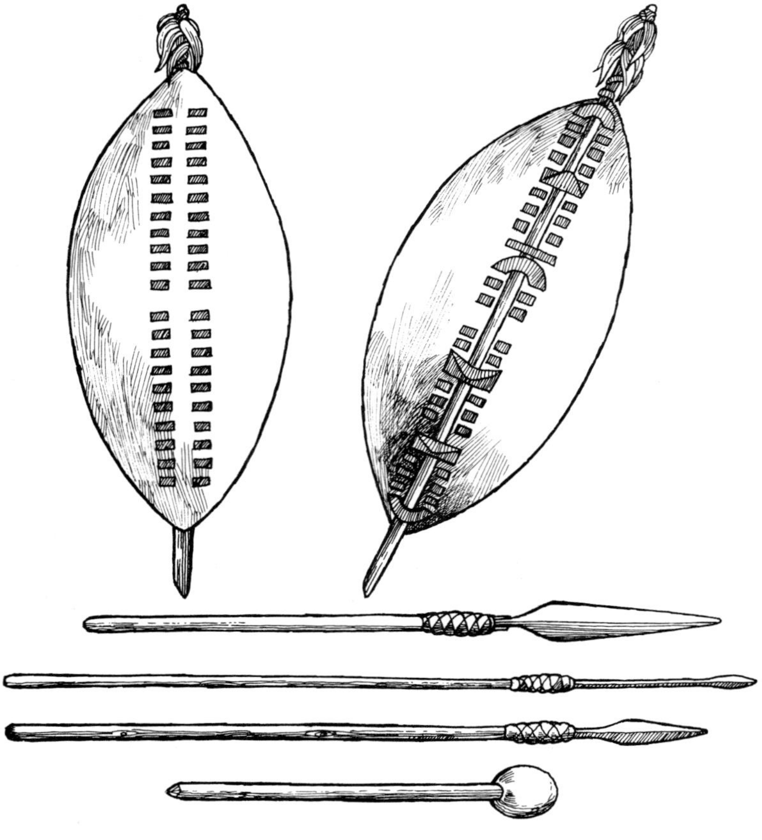

Ndebele spears and shields

INVOICE

NATIONAL MUSEUMS & MONUMENTS OF ZIMBABWE

15 - 9 - 1987

M

GZ № 25672

	1	MTC @ 825		8	25
				8	25

6.4 *Isika*

This is a short stabbing weapon with a 15 cm blade and a shaft 45 cm long. The spear blade is set into the wooden shaft and secured by means of metal bands or animal sinew. The weapon is delicately balanced and only a master craftsman skilled in the manufacture of spears can produce the correctly proportioned weapon.[18]

18 Summers R. and Pagden p.20

6.5 *Usiba*

Similar to the *isika* this weapon is also used in a stabbing manner. Generally it has a much shorter 10 cm blade and a longer shaft up to 69 cm.[19]

19 Ibid

6.6 *Isishula*

The *isishula* spear has an 8 cm blade which extends from the end of an iron tang some 12 cm long which is set into a wooden shaft approximately 60 cm in length. The *isishula* spear probably came into the Ndebele armoury through contact with the Shona who used this type of throwing spear to hunt wild animals.[20]

20 Ibid

6.7 *Manufacture of spears*

Very few of the genuine *isika* spears which originated in Natal now exist. Most of them were either re-ground and re-set after they had been damaged in fighting. By so doing, they lost much of the original craftmanship. A few very old examples of the *isika* stabbing spear are said to be in the possession of some Ndebele families in the Nkayi district where they are treasured as family heirlooms.[21]

21 Ibid p.23

It must be remembered that the original Zulu design differed from the Shona type spear head with a half-hollow cross section (see spears under Shona). Shona spear technology was gradually adopted by the Ndebele who were never truly skilled in the art of metal work and relied heavily on Shona blacksmiths for their iron. Some Ndebele smiths *(amahole)* did become quite adept in the operation of furnaces and forges but it is most likely that they acquired this skill from the Shona. One of the most important centres of Ndebele iron work was located in the Malungwane Hills near Esikhoveni.[22]

22 Ibid p.23

6.8 *The spear in Shona society (Pfumo or Mapfumo)*

The Ndebele spear was a relatively recent addition to the material culture of Zimbabwe as the spear has been known to the Shona for centuries before. One of the earliest written references to ths spear in warfare comes from Portuguese records of the sixteenth century, when they were used during a battle between the forces of the Munhumutapa, and the invading Portuguese under the command of Francisco Barreto. During the course of this battle, warriors of the Munhumutapa threw their darts, which they called Pomberar. The Portuguese rallied their forces and counter attacked in the face of stiff opposition which was put up with bows and arrows and assegais but the day was finally lost to the superior firepower of the Portuguese artillery and muskets.[23]

23 Couto, Diogo do. Documents on the Portuguese, 1962. Cap. 25 Vol. VIII p. 289.

Descriptions of the Shona speaking people of the Manica region show how warriors were armed with spears or assegais.

Ndebele warrior showing spear and shield

People described as being 'Mocaranga' made great use of this weapon in their struggles against the Portuguese.[24]

24 Couto, Diogo pp. 249-323.

6.9 *The shona spear*

The essential difference between the Ndebele and Shona spear is that the Ndebele assegai was used as a stabbing weapon rather than as a throwing spear. Later, Shona influences led the Ndebele to use the larger throwing spear.

Amongst the Shona, the size of the blade and length of the shaft differ from region to region and depend on the intended use of the weapon. Heavy broad bladed spears were used for hunting large antelope or hippos. Others, with barbs were used for fishing.

6.10 *Description of the Shona spear*

In most cases, the weapon consisted of an iron blade which is set into a suitable wooden shaft of a certain length. The opposite tang is made with a point and heated red hot before being driven into the shaft. The join is reinforced with iron binding *(nyenza)*. In many Shona spears the weapon is fitted with a blunt tool at the other end. This *(nzope)* permits the weapon to be stuck into the ground in an upright position until ready for use.[25] The *nzope* is also used as a digging tool for unearthing roots or vlei tubers *(hota)* which are edible or medicinal.[26]

25 Snowden A.E. Some Technological Notes on Weapons and Implements used in Mashonaland, Nada, No. 17 1940.

26 Chinhoyi, Nhira Nzvere (born c. 1870) Oral History N.A.Z. for an interesting description of how the Chihota people derived their name, i.e. by digging for the Hota Vlei tuber with the nzope digging fixture on the spear.

6.11 *Manufacture of the Shona spear*

In order to make a spear head the iron was first beaten out into thin strips. Two of these strips were cut into the required length and then welded together in the forge.

The overlapping parts were then hammered down sufficiently to leave a narrow groove along the blade on either side causing the edges to be on slightly different planes thereby creating the typical half hollow cross section. Upon their arrival in Western Zimbabwe, the people of Mzilikazi made good use of skilled Shona blacksmiths and metal craftsmen. As the two cultures started to mix, the Ndebele began to rely heavily on Shona smiths to make their spears and change in style.

7 Shields (*Isihlangu* or *Ihawu*)

In the context of Ndebele culture, the spear must be considered in close association with the ox hide shields (*isihlangu*) which served to protect its wearer and as a means of regimental identification was of the greatest importance in Ndebele military society in the last century. The makers of shields (*umsikiwezinhlangu*) were considered to be craftsmen of great distinction. It was their task to select the skins, prepare them, and cut them to the required pattern. The work of the *umsikiwezinhlangu* was monitored by the regimental quarter masters (*umhloliwezinhlangu*), who inspected the shields before they were submitted to the King for his final scrutiny.[27] There were two different types of shields: the first was carried by youngsters herding cattle or by messengers sent out on errands by the King. It was smaller than the war shield, which was only used on special occasions such as the annual ceremony of *inxwala*, for war, or when the men danced before the King during military reviews.[28]

27 Jones, Dr Neville, My Friend Kumalo, pp. 51-52.

28 Summers and Pagden, The Warriors, pp. 24-25-26. See also David Carnegie, 1882.

7.1 *Manufacture of shields*

Specially selected oxen provided the hides from which shields were manufactured. This task was left to the master shield maker (*umsikiwezinhlangu*) who prepared the ox hide in the following manner. A selected skin was put into a river at sunset and left to soak overnight until the following morning when it was removed, washed and cleaned. Thereafter the skin was buried in a cattle kraal and allowed to become thoroughly softened by the mixture of dung and mud. After being cured in the dung it was further softened using a wooden mallet. Now the ox skin was ready to be cut out into the required oval shape measuring 95-100 cm long and 35 cm wide with the skin facing outwards. The skin was secured to a stick with animal skin ornament on top.[29]

29 Ibid

In two parallel vertical lines running down the middle, small holes were cut, through which strips of soft, different coloured skin were drawn. This served to introduce the correct pattern denoting the regimental insignia and badge of rank of the owner.[30]

30 Ibid

The shield maker was considered to be a highly skilled and competent craftsman and he was well respected in his society.[31]

31 Ibid

7.2 *Insignia and badge of rank*

Once shields had been passed by the King it was the regimental *Induna* who allocated choice of skins to the bravest men of his *impi*. In most cases the honourable colour was white, into which a little black or brown was introduced. Regiments under training used black coloured shields. [32] [33]

32 Ibid

33 Jones, Dr Neville, see appendix 2 for list of Ndebele regiments.

7.3 Decline in technology

In 1893 it was noted that many of the Ndebele shields had already undergone a marked deterioration when compared with shields of similar age from Zululand. It follows that today almost no examples of authentic shields survive other than the few collected by museums. Small symbolic shields are still made in Matabeleland for use in ceremonies and for the tourist trade.

7.4 The Shona shields

The Shona armies of the sixteenth century were equipped with shields said to be as tall as a man and some three palms in width (24 cm). These were made of wood lattice or wicker work with a spike at the bottom.[34]

34 Beach, D. N., The Shona and Zimbabwe, Mambo, 1980 Cap. 3. p. 105 (see also Gomes, Viagem (1648 pp. 206-207).

8 Clubs and knobkerries

Knobkerries or clubs featuring the brass or copper wire work

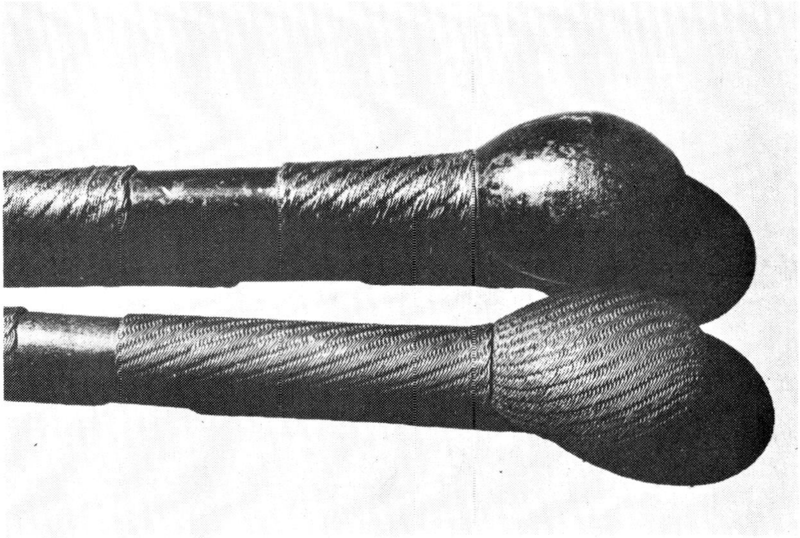

The Shona knobkerrie *tsvimbo* has been largely superceded by the more stylized version which is commonly found in Zimbabwe today. But during the sixteenth century, warriors of the Munhumutupa carried a good variety of weapons including a *simbo* which was described as a short club with a bludgeon shaped end and which was the last weapon they (the Shona soldiers) threw in battle.[35]

35 Monclaro, Francisco de, Documents on the Portuguese, Vol. VIII, cap. 26, p. 379. The term 'Simbo' could well be a dialectic variant of the modern Shona Tsvimbo meaning club or stick.

Wooden clubs are carved from a single piece of heavy grained wood. The head of the club is usually formed by a knot in the wood. The handle of the weapon can be decorated with copper or brass wire and in some cases the scrotum of a large antelope or ox is shrunk over the clubhead.

Some but not all of the Ndebele carried the knobkerrie (*induku*). The weapon has been pictured in early illustrations of Ndebele warriors attending the *inxwala* ceremony in the 1880s. There is also evidence that the *induku* was used as part of the Ndebele soldiers weaponry and was used in hand to hand fighting.[36]

36 Child, H. The History of the Ndebele, (former Rhodesia Ministry of Internal Affairs publication 1968.)

Clubs

9 Iron smelting

The people of pre-colonial Zimbabwe had, for a long time, the technology necessary for iron smelting and smithwork.

Examination of archaeological and geological sites throughout the country confirm this fact. Before the arrival of the Portuguese on the east coast of Africa in 1498, the Arabic-Swahili traders were actually exporting iron ore via the Port of Sofala. Iron smelting was carried out at various locations throughout the country including Chilimanzi, Mount Buhwa (site of the major ore source for the modern Zimbabwe Iron and Steel Corporation works at Kwekwe), the Matopo hills, the Zambezi valley and at sites near Redcliff. However, the art of iron smelting appears to have been highly developed by the Njanja people settled on the eastern banks of the Sabi river lying in the shadow of the Wedza mountains. The Njanja technology flourished and reached a peak some 50 years before the establishment of the B.S.A. Co. administration. The ore or *mhangura* was taken from the twin mines of Gandamasunga and Chipangure which were effectively controlled by the Mbire. In order to get their ore, and ferry it across the Sabi to their forges, the Njanja were obliged to pay tribute in the form of manufactured implements — hoes and spears. Of the items fashioned by the Njanja, the badza *(hoe)* was perhaps the most important because of its varied application in agriculture, mining and value as dowry. The value of the *badza* was later replaced by cattle but the term *badza* is still synonymous with cattle when considered in the context of *roora* (bride payment to the parents).

The Njanja dynasty has an interesting history and according to legend amongst people of the Wedza/Sabi area, the clan was founded by one Muroro. Muroro was a trader from Tete, who, whilst trading in the Wedza area sometime around 1750 fell ill. He was nursed back to health, but having been abandoned for dead by his companions, he became assimilated and married into a local family. From this union sprang the Njanja dynasty. This legend is supported by the fact that the Njanja *mutupo* is Moyo, their Chidao is Sinyoro (a phonetic variation of Senhor in much the same manner as *fodya* is a deviation of folha or leaf from tobacco in Portuguese).[37]

37 Chigwedere, A. Interview, March, 1982

Weapons and implements manufactured by the Njanja and others included the hoes *(badza)*, spears *(pfumo)*, arrowheads *(musewe)*, axe *(gano)*, battle axe *(humbwa)*, adze *(mbezo)*, wood axe *(demo)*, dagger *(bakatwa)*, digging tool or spear *(nzope)* and ringlets of miniature spear heads which were used as backscratchers and ornaments.

Shona metal workers: the woodworker on the right is making axe and hoe handles while the smith in the middle is beating out a hoe blade

Iron furnace: the mixture of iron ore and charcoal are added to the furnace which bears the symbolic breasts and abdominal markings. Two assistants operate the goat skin belows fuelling the fire with oxygen

'Traditional' iron smelting set into rapid decline following the introduction of 20th century technology and the import of cheaper mass produced agricultural and general purpose implements. Indigenous iron smelting was viewed as uneconomic and quaint by the administration. During the early days of the B.S.A. Co. administration, surviving smiths were trotted around the countryside to demonstrate their craft. A permanent exhibit was later established at the Queen Victoria Museum in Harare and this featured the most celebrated of the demonstrators, Ranga, and the Njanja techniques.[38]

All furnaces followed the same basic design. Constructed of hardened clay containing refractory properties, the furnace had an opening at either end with a central overhead chimney. Bellows made from the skin of a complete goat were attached to one end to introduce oxygen to fuel the charcoal fires into which the ore mixture was placed. It has been said that the *mavira* or furnace symbolised the female body with the molten iron ore opening representing the vulva giving life to the iron.

The Njanja iron industry has been described as being perhaps the most remarkable of pre-colonial industries in Zimbabwe which died partly by administrative action, but principally in the face of overwhelming competition from outside. Finally, for their cooperation during the rising of 1896-97 the Njanja were rewarded by being even more confined in their Sabi north reserve, when the ruling 'Native Commissioner' Posselt moved in a branch of their traditional enemies, the Hera, from appropriated land in the early 1920s.[39] After this, their craft disappeared quickly.

38 Mackenzie, J. Njanja Iron Trade, Nada, 1975 p. 207.

39 Ibid p. 20

The blacksmiths craft was practised in Matabeleland although they relied greatly on Shona craftsmen to provide them with their weapons and iron tools.Their furnaces were similar to those used by the Shona, i.e. resembling the female torso with the two small breasts. The pig iron was then beaten before being re-heated and by a process of much hammering and heating, good malleable iron was produced and made into spear heads, axes, hoes, adzes, knives and other tools. As in the Shona speaking regions, this craft disappeared rapidly due to cheaper and better steel imports.[40]

40 Jones, Dr Neville, My Friend Kumalo, etc. pp. 102-104 on Ndebele Iron Craft.

10 Gun powder and muzzle loaders (zvigidi)

The guns that were imported to Zimbabwe and exchanged for trade goods became highly prized possessions. They were useful for hunting as well as being far more effective as weapons of war. During the 19th century, the Shona made copies of these imported weapons, and these became known by the onomatopoeic names *zvigidi* or *chigidi* (from the sound of firing). These weapons were used extensively and effectively in the Chindunduma of 1896 (the first Chimurenga war).

10.1 Gun powder manufacture

The *chigidi* was a most unpredictable weapon, liable to blow up in the face of the unfortunate user. Gunpowder was very scarce but soon the innovative Shona were able to develop their own supplies. Who exactly discovered the secret of locally manufactured gunpowder will perhaps never be known but *unga* (powder)[41] was certainly produced. Soil from granite kopje caves, where rock dassies *(Hyrax procaviidae)* can be found was gathered, boiled and filtered in order to extract salt-petre which was then combined with ground up charcoal. This elementary form of gunpowder was frequently used in the *chigidi* and *pani* muzzle loaders.[42]

Following the failure of the first Chimurenga and the subjugation of the Shona, the British South Africa Company Police had rounded up rebel villagers and their weapons confiscated. However, not all weapons were confiscated and some people were permitted to licence their weapons officially.[43]

The manufacture of the *chigidi* was a remarkable innovation improved with time. It can be compared with earlier technological achievements in mining, smelting, agriculture, not to mention ample evidence of the steadily evolving culture and a democratic way of life. All this is in contrast with later political and racist propaganda that the Shona people were helplessly primitive and needed to be protected and civilized.

41 Vambe L. An Ill Fated People, Heineman, 1972, pp. 50-51.

42 Kaprio Chisvo (born c. 1868-78), Oral Records, NAZ.

43 The Njanja were not officially disarmed until 1913; by 1930-31 thousands of weapons were still licenced in the Victoria Province (Masvingo Prov.).

10.2 Manufacture of ammunition

The Ndebele also made effective use of European guns during the late nineteenth century and certainly during the risings in Matabeleland. They had soon discovered to their cost that assegais were no match for guns. But having acquired the European guns and blunderbusses they found that ammunition was not always available. This lead to an interesting technological development when the Ndebele started to manufacture their own bullets. Bullets were moulded for use in the Lee Metford and Martini-Henry rifles. A reed of the required bore was chosen and the pith removed. Lead was melted and poured into the reed mould. The circular reed moulds produced some very passable bullets.[44] In other extreme cases, fragments of quartz with lead around them, glass stoppers from soda pop bottles, curb chains, pot legs, stones and pebbles encased in lead served as bullets. These bullets did terrible damage to human tissue and generally resulted in the amputation of limbs.[45]

44 Sykes, Frank W., With Plummer in Matabeleland, Books of Rhodesia, 1972, p. 123.

45 Ibid pp. 249-253.

10.3 Umbhobho Womgqitshwa, an Ndebele gun

Armourers and smiths attached to the elite Insukamini Regiment of the Ndebele were able to supplement the supply of weapons by making their own guns during the 1890s. It was extremely simple in that it comprised a length of steel tube which was attached to a wooden stock. This join was reinforced by shrinking wet hide over the two components. In shape and size, the weapon resembled the Martini-Henry but differed in that it had no trigger. The firing mechanism consisted of a small hole which was primed with gunpowder just before firing.

The barrel needed packing with a wild shrub known as *ububende*. It was gathered and used in a fresh state; under pressure the herb proved highly inflamable. Once the barrel had been loaded about 90% full, the bullet, consisting of a smooth or rounded pebble was finally rammed hard against the compressed shrub. If gunpowder was available, some was poured into the priming hole and ignited by striking flints — *idotshi* to produce a spark. The dry powder mechanism was enough to ignite the compressed leaves which then burned under tremendous pressure. As the inflamable material burned, gases built up under pressure resulting in explosive release driving the bullet out at great speed.

The firer would be able to judge the burning time and take aim against his chosen target in sufficient time. According to oral tradition, this gun was powerful enough to fell even large game such as antelope as well as large carnivores. Hunting was strictly regulated and carried out only on the orders of the King whose royal armourers kept these weapons when they were not required.[46]

46 Interview with Tshabalala whose father served with the elite Insukamini Regiment in the 1890s. National Museums and Monuments, Central Region, Gweru, 8.6.83. Asst. Technical Officer, Mr L. Nyoni.

5 Musical instruments

1 A short history of music in Zimbabwe

During the final phase of the Chimurenga war of liberation 1972-1980, the *Mbira,* with other instruments, played a vital role as a medium for traditional folk compositions such as the Mandarendare and Nyamaropa which were decisive in raising the morale and spirit of the soldiers going into battle against the enemy. Played at Pungwes[1] and other gatherings, they served as exhortations to fight the enemy well. These and other compositions were performed during the struggle to liberate Zimbabwe.

There can be no doubt that Zimbabwean music suffered a decline during the dark days of the colonial era. In keeping with the paternalism of western attitudes of the time, 'Native' musical instruments were regarded as primitive, crude or simple, not being able to produce music (acceptable to Western cultural ears) as a pure and aesthetic art form. Olaf Axelsson of the Kwanongoma College of Music in Bulawayo observes of African music that:

> '. . . it follows its own rules which need have no similarities to Western music, and which therefore make it a true and indigenous art form, an art form which has a direct impact on the society in which it lives, fulfilling a functional aspect of daily life which man cannot live without.'[2]

He continues:

> '. . . the same is true of African musical instruments, built according to the technology of their society to produce sounds which are of great fascination and apt for their environment.'

This is certainly true of Zimbabwean musical instruments. Axelsson also noted that:

> 'African musical instruments have slowly disappeared from ordinary life and those instruments which are still being used are more or less regarded as museum pieces of a long-gone past.'

The African musicologist Hugh Tracey has written that:

1 Pungwe: An institution developed during the liberation war 1972-80 possibly named after the Pungwe river which flowed near the Nyadzonia refugee camp which was the scene of a massacre during the war. Pungwes were all-night ceremonies of dance and song where guerrillas and peasants expressed their dedication to the struggle through songs such as Kana Pfuti Dzichirira, Zimbabwe Nyika Yavatema, Muka and Nzira Dzemasoja Dzokuzvibata Nadzo and many others.Before the liberation war of 1972-1980, the term 'Pungwe' was already in use (by 1967 the term was in use) particulary in urban areas where it referred to all night disco shows frequented by teenagers. Origin has a lot to do with the ideophone, Ngwe (light again after darkness).

2 O. Axelsson, Notes on African musical instruments, Art Zimbabwe, 1982, p. 81.

> 'The African who comes into contact with European music does so at a great disadvantage. He is faced with an art form representing two centuries accumulation of written music of the western world. He is persuaded, moreover, by the minor exponents of this foreign music that his own culture is barbaric and insignificant and should be jettisoned in favour of the European style which has so strong an associative power in the minds of his teacher.'

Tracey continues in his assertion that:

> '. . . the folk music of one village or at most one district, is rarely ever analysed by its exponents, although unwritten, is the natural expression of the musical (and cultural) emotions of the people from day to day.'[3]

Despite influence of Western civilization and its own cultural value, Zimbabwe's musical instruments and tradition have managed to survive. The modern popularity of the *mbira*, the *ngoma* and the *marimba* are examples of this. However, not all Zimbabwean musical instruments enjoy such popularity and many have disappeared from everyday life. So we might say that many of the instruments described in this chapter are nothing more than interesting museum pieces, but this is not true at all. Each instrument, in varying degrees of importance, continues to play a role in the cultural lives of the people, although on a decreasing scale. By reviving the knowledge and use of these lesser known instruments this trend can be reversed and apparent museum oddities will once again be able to take their place alongside their more popular counterparts in the contemporary music of Zimbabwe.

It is sensible to start with the Mbira, one of the most popular instruments in Zimbabwe. The *mbira* belongs to the ideophone group of instruments and it is believed to have developed from one original instrument invented more than 1 000 years ago.[4]

The *mbira* is certainly the instrument:

> '. . . they call *a mbira* made from iron, being composed of narrow flat rods of iron about a palm in length tempered in the fire so that each has a different sound.'

This instrument was referred to by the Dominican father João dos Santos who roamed amongst Shona speaking people around 1586.

> 'There are only nine of these rods, placed in a row close together, with the ends nailed to a piece of wood like a bridge of a violin. The player strikes the loose ends of the rods with their thumb nails, which they allow to grow for that purpose, and they strike the keys as lightly as a good player strikes those of the harpsicord, producing altogether a sweet and gentle harmony of accordant sounds.'[5]

3 Hugh Tracey, African music, a modern view, Nada, 1942.

4 The date and place of invention of the Mbira has not been precisely determined. Some speculation suggests it was devised in Zimbabwe about 1 000 years ago. The Mbira type instrument can be found in a number of African countries. It is possible that the instrument came to Zimbabwe during the early Bantu migration. There is some oral legend suggesting the Mbira was invented in Zimbabwe but there is no definite proof of this.

5 Santos, João dos, Ethiopia Oriental (Evora 1609), 2 Vol. I and II, Lisbon reprint 1892 translations of Theal.

Mbira

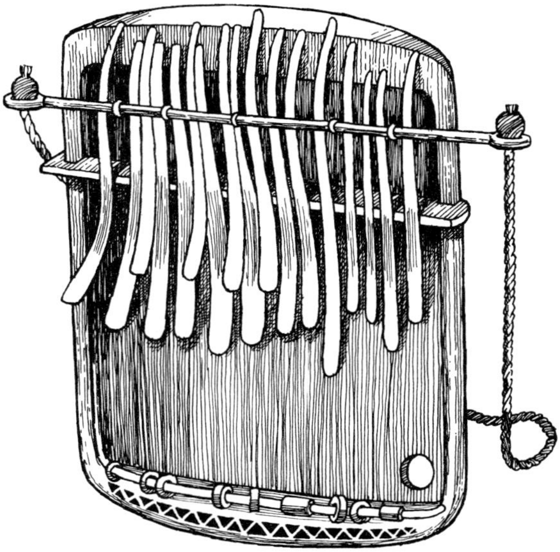

More recently, the German geologist Karl Gottlieb Maunch visited Zimbabwe in the 19th century when he sketched a *mbira* in use. His sketch done in 1872 shows a *mbira* with seven more keys than those commonly used today. This was probably the *njari* which has anything between 29 and 34 keys according to regional differences. (See illustration of Karl Maunch's *mbira*.) Artist and explorer Thomas Baines, in 1860, whilst journeying up the Zambezi, made a water colour of a *mbira* which is now identified as being the *hera* or *matepe* or *sansi* which has up to 37 keys and is popular among the people of Tete region and also the vaKorekore of N.E. Zimbabwe.

Mbiras in Zimbabwe fall into five or six categories and are described as follows:

2 Ideophones or percussion instruments

2.1 *The mbira of the ancestoral spirits (Mbira dza vadzimu)*

These generally have from 22 to 24 keys mounted on a wooden soundboard which has a finger hole in the lower right hand corner. The keys of this type of *mbira* are wider and thicker than those of other Shona *mbira*, and whereas many other *mbira* have two rows of keys across the soundboard, the *Mbira dza vadzimu* is different in that it has two rows on the left hand side and one on the right side. This type of *mbira* was played solely for religious ceremonies and other rituals for the spirits, hence its

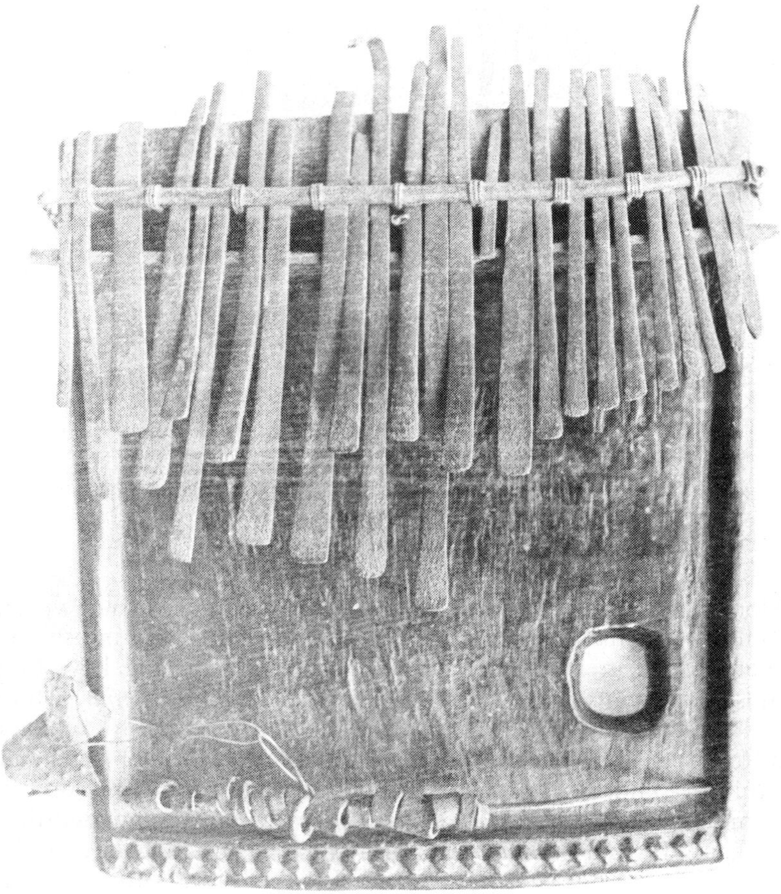

Mbira dzavadzimu: these pianos are very interesting specimens of primitive musical art; they have thirty or more iron keys, arranged to scale, fixed onto a piece of wood about half a foot square, which is decorated with carving behind. This instrument they generally put into a gourd, with pieces of bone around the edge to increase the sound, which is decidedly melodious and recalls a spinet

name. This instrument, as with all others, with the exception of the *mbira dza vaTonga*, is played inside a gourd or *deze* which acts as a resonator. The musician takes his *deze* (calabash), and props the *mbira* inside with two pieces of stick wedged firmly against the insides of the gourd. If the *mbira* is not correctly wedged, it will not resonate properly. The player then sits with the calabash on his knees and starts *kukwenya mbira* which means to scratch or tickle the *mbira*. This is the common expression for playing the instrument. A *mbira* player is known as *Gwenyambira*.

2.2 *Matepe mbira*

This instrument is said to have originated in Mozambique or possibly other countries to the North. Around the Tete district of Mozambique it is known as the *sansa* or *sansi* and this is certainly the instrument João dos Santos wrote about in 1586. This instrument is common in Zimbabwe with its related instruments of the *hera* and *munyonga mbira*. The keys which range from 29 to 34 (or even up to 52 plus) are arranged on three rows or manuals. The keys are thin, narrow and long and have an upward curve which bend away from the hollowed out soundboard. The soundboard has metal (brass or copper) beads mounted on a thin rod inside the hollow of the board acting as vibrators and this is fixed to a plate on the surface of the soundboard. These vibrators as with those of the *mbira dza vadzimu* were traditionally made from snail shells or pieces of ant-eater scale. Bottle tops have replaced the old snail shells and appear to resonate just as well, if not better.

2.3 *Njari mbira*

This is possibly a later introduction into southern Zimbabwe at about the end of the 19th century and has keys evenly placed in only two rows or manuals across the tray shaped soundboard. The average maximum number of keys is 34 the size and shape of which are similar to a Matepe and its variations.

2.4 *Mbira dza vaNdau*

As the name implies, this type of musical instrument is found in the eastern districts of Zimbabwe (around Chipinge) and is very common amongst the Ndau people. Thin keys are arranged on two manuals numbering from 29 to 31, also on a tray shaped soundboard. Whilst most Shona Mbiras have deeper keys located in the middle of the keyboard and with scales ascending outward, the *mbira dza vaNdau* is different in that the lower keys are on the left with the higher keys ascending to the right of the soundboard, as on European keyboard.

2.5 *Mbira dza vaTonga*

As indicated by its name this instrument is popular amongst the Tonga people of the Zambezi Valley in Zimbabwe. The instrument is generally smaller and more rounded than other Zimbabwean *mbira*. Between eight and fourteen keys are mounted on a small wooden soundboard with a circular hole. The instrument is hand held and played over a gourd or tin which serves as the resonator. The *mbira dzavaTonga* is often used to play an interesting modern adaptation of an ancient ceremony with more sinister connotations. The modern version is similar to 'pin the tail on the donkey' game in which the blindfolded player must correctly locate the position of a chosen object by following the subtle tonal change of the music as the player approaches or moves away from the chosen item.

According to legend this 'game' was played or enacted long ago in order to point out evil or ill intentioned people in the village.

2.6 *Karimba Mbira*

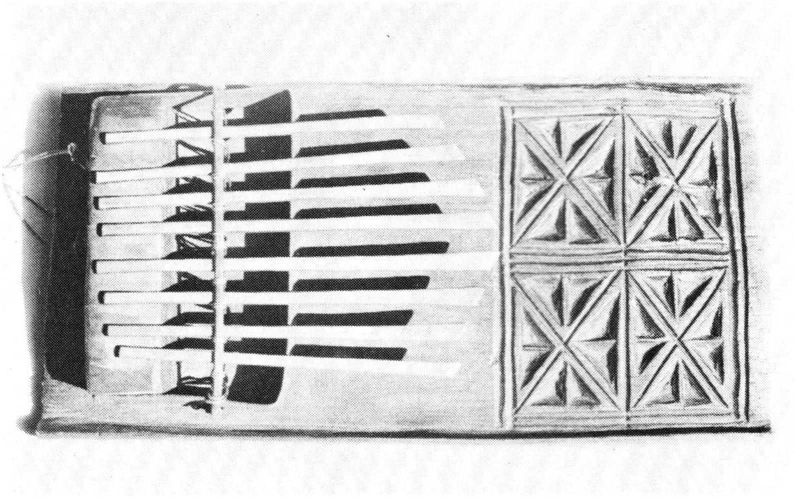

Kalimba type *mbira*

The Karimba *mbira* and a popular variety known as the Ndimba are small *mbira* with keys numbering from 8 to 12 arranged in one row across a wooden soundboard. This type is played only for entertainment. Interestingly, this instrument might well be the most similar to the original *mbira* believed to have been invented in Zimbabwe some 1 000 years ago. Although not so common in Zimbabwe, it has spread to Zambia and is found in the western province there. The well known authority on Zimbabwean musicology, Hugh Tracey, developed a recent Zimbabwean Karimba which is based on this design but different in that it has a hollow chamber beneath the top soundboard upon which the eight to twelve keys are arranged. A small opening allows the sound to resonate in the chamber. This instrument is popular nowadays and is easy to play.

2.7 *The deze or calabash*

This is the resonator with vibrators arranged in rows around the outside of the gourd opening. These vibrators were traditionally made from snail, tortoise, scally pangolin or sea shells but today they are made from bottle tops which are more durable and easily available. The old fashioned calabashes were often decorated with designs and patterns.

In considering non-Zimbabwean *mbira* it is important to remember that this ideophone can be found in many other African countries. In Angola, for example, there is the Kissanji, which is virtually identical to the Mozambique *sansi* or our own *Matepe mbira*. In Mozambique the most widely distributed instrument is the six or seven key *sansi* or *chitata*. This instrument is similar to the *Mbira dzavaTonga* in that it is held over the opening of a calabash during playing, but here the calabash is much larger and fitted with vibrating shells or bottle tops whereas the Tonga variety is not. The Mozambique Phiane or Birimbau de Boca (mouth mbira) is another version of the Mbira. It is not as widespread as the *sansi* or *chitata* but has an unusual construction. Essential to the instrument is the soundboard where the metal keys are separated into two groups, six or seven keys on either side of a series of small holes drilled into the board. It seems that the player holds the instrument against his mouth which acts as a resonating chamber.

The *mbira* of all varieties, in Mozambique as in Zimbabwe, is played to traditional songs rich in history and folk lore. Oral historians have always used the *mbira* compositions as the base for their stories. There is a particularly lovely *mbira* composition in Mozambique which is a funeral song for a dead child.[6]

Inevitably, traditional music like any other music undergoes the process of change. Such developments are found in the work of a well known Harare Gwenyambira, Mr David Gweshe,[7] a 40-year-old traditionalist who also dances and dramatises stories of Africa's past. He started playing the Mbira in 1961 having inherited knowledge and inspiration from his parents and ancestors. He has developed a 58 key *mbira* which is probably unique in Africa. David Gweshe explained at the unveiling of his new *mbira* in 1981 that the art of its manufacture was learnt by his ancestors a long time ago — even before the advent of the iron technology. At that time they used to cut bamboo into thin rods and use them as keys, he said. David Gweshe was appointed by the Ministry of Education as co-instructor to the National Dance Company, a traditional group formed in 1981.

6 Martinho lutero Domingo, Instrumentos musicais de Mozambique, 25.4.82.

7 The Sunday Mail, 22nd November, 1981.

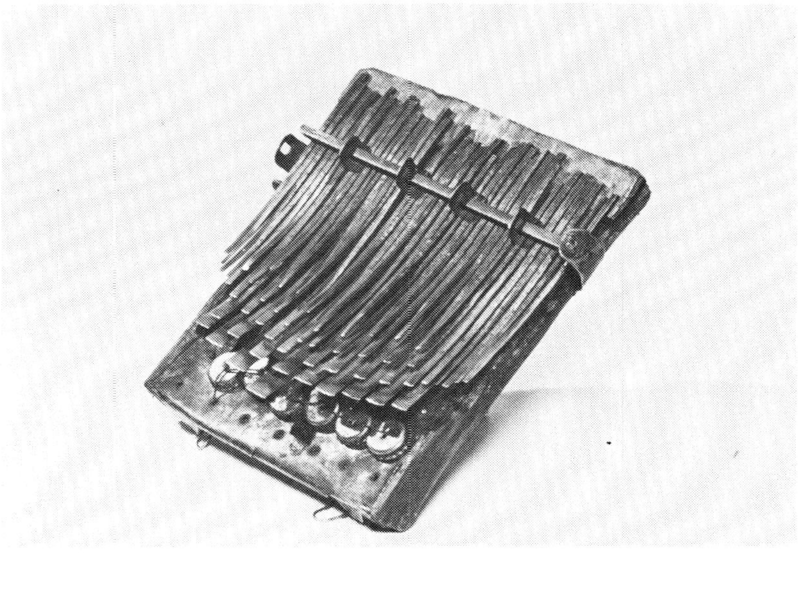

The 56-key *mbira* devised by David Gweshe

2.8 *The varimba or marimba (xylophone)*

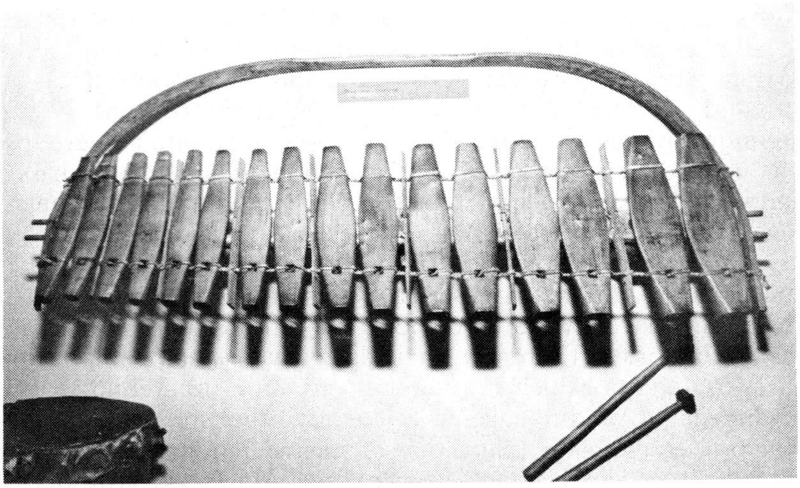

Marimba (xylophone)

This tuned ideophone, similar to a xylophone, is easily accepted by the 'western' ear, and has enjoyed popularity as western musical ideas are adopted in Zimbabwe music. The Marimba was already known in the early days of the Zimbabwe State and was certainly played at the court of Great Zimbabwe. Father Joao dos Santos commented on the instrument which he found in usage amongst the 'Macaranga' in 1586. He wrote:

> '. . . the best and most musical of their instruments is composed[8] of long gourds held close together and arranged in order. Upon the mouths of these gourds, keys of thin wood are suspended. The musicians play upon the keys with sticks. At the point of these instruments are buttons of sinews rolled into a tight ball. Striking the notes with these two sticks the blows resound in the mouths of the gourds producing a sweet and rhythmic harmony, which can be heard as far as the sound of a good harpsicord.'[9]

Recently, it has been developed and became known as the neo-Zimbabwean *marimba,* an instrument which is enjoying great popularity. Developments have shown that plastic hollow tubes are as good as the traditional gourds as resonators.

In Mozambique, the *marimba* is a very popular instrument. It is known as the *mbila, varimba,* or *makwilo* and variations of this xylophone can be found throughout the country. The most popular is the *mbila*. The name *mbila* serves both the instrument itself and the dance which accompanies it. In Mozambique, the *mbila* has the same cultural and social role as the *mbira* does in Zimbabwe.

In the far east, this xylophone is commonly found in most orchestras. Some students of music claim that the *marimba* originates in the far east (particularly Indonesia) and that it was

8 In the original text of Fr. Joao dos Santos, the ambira is apparently confused with the Mbira. Here he refers to the Mbila or Marimba, xylophone.

9 Santos, João dos.

introduced to Europe by travellers and explorers. Much earlier the *marimba* is believed to have been introduced to the coast of Mozambique around two thousand years ago when some Indonesian voyagers established a settlement in the vicinity of Inhambane (some 400 km north of Maputo).

To make a good *mbira* or *marimba* requires much skill and technology. For example, only a special type of wood will adequately serve as the keys and this timber can only be found in the Inhambane region of Mozambique — the *mwenje* tree.[10] This wood has certain unique qualities of resonance suitable to the *mbila*. Mozambique workers who went to work on the South African gold mines constructed *mbila* out of woods locally available, but maintain that the sounds thus produced were not as good as those produced by the Mozambique *mwenje* wood.

10 Muenje — probably Mushenje, a very hard wood commonly used for this purpose in Zimbabwe. Mukamba is also used for the same purpose.

The characteristic sound of the *mbila* or *timbila* (pl) of Mozambique is produced by resonators (bottle gourds) suspended beneath the key board. Suitable bottle gourds are selected, carefully emptied, cleaned and cut to provide two openings, one at either end. One end allows the sound to enter and the other, that which allows the sound to escape, is covered with a thin membrane of animal skin. Sound, having been produced when the wooden key is struck vibrates through this membrane producing the 'tone' so characteristic of the Mozambique instrument. For each different sized wooden key, there is a correspondingly proportioned bottle gourd suspended beneath it joined to the body of the instrument by a special beeswax taken from hives made in the ground. Without all these important details, the instrument will not produce the correct tone.

Single key *marimba*

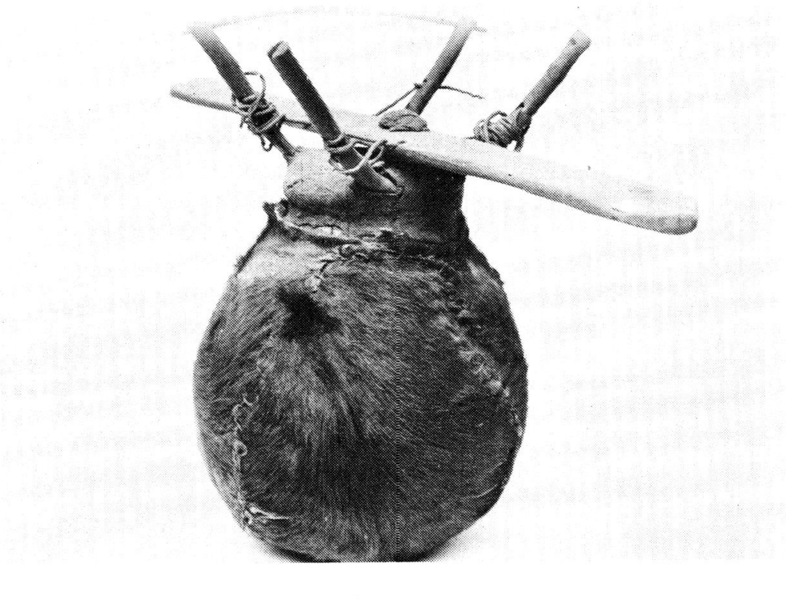

2.9 *Hosho*

Another Zimbabwean ideophone is the *hosho* or hand-held rattles usually made from the dried shell of the wild orange *matamba* which is filled with small river pebbles or *hota*[11] seeds. A short length of wood forms as the handle. A development or perhaps earlier example of the *hosho* is the vegetable pumpkin (*mapudzi*), which often grows into the shape of an ideal *hosho*. The gourd is emptied of the seeds, filled with *hota* or river pebbles and plugged. *Hosho* are played in pairs, one in each hand, in cross rhythms.

11 Musonza, P. M., Oral Records, National Archives, April, 1982 (born c. 1886).

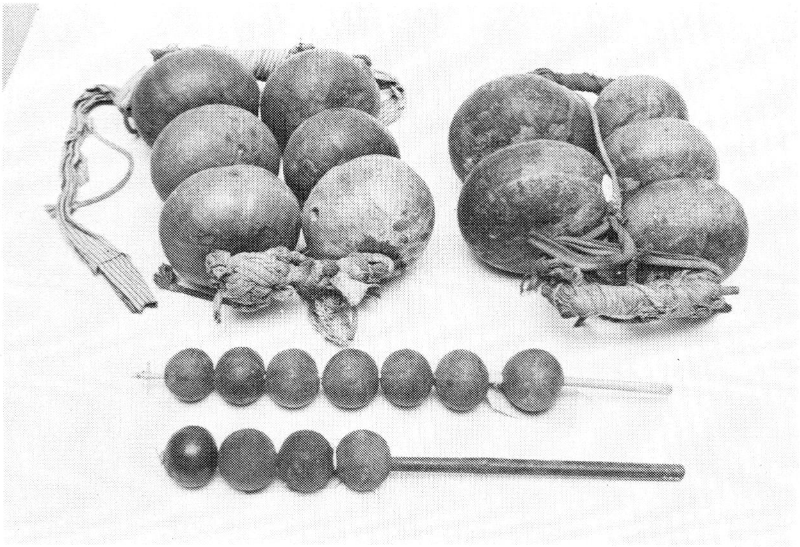

Magagada (leg) and *hosho* (hand rattles)

2.10 *Magagada and magavhu*

The *magagada* rattles are similar to the *hosho* and are also ideophones. The *magagada* consists of a number of empty dry *mapudzi* or *shwawu* marrows filled with *hota* seeds and arranged in series of six or eight according to size as leg rattles. Joined together by *mupfuti* bark fibre the *magagada* are tied to the ankles of dancers and accompany the rhythm of the dance. They are usually found in concert with *hosho* and *ngoma*.

2.11 *Mahlwayi*

Similar to the *magagada* leg rattles are the Ndebele *mahlwayi* leg rattles made from ilala palm fronds to form small casings for seeds, or small pebbles. Dozens of these rattles are threaded on a long piece of string which are wrapped round the dancers leg. The *mahlwayi* are very common in the Plumtree area.

Mahlwayi (leg rattles)

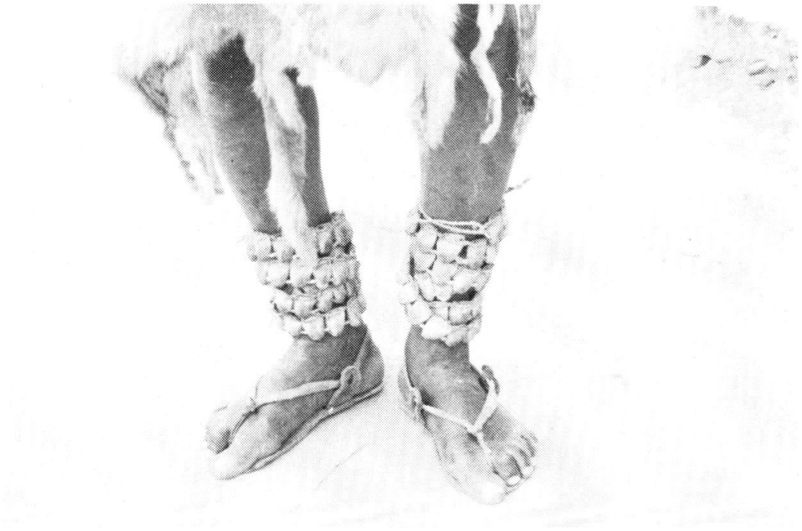

2.12 *Majaka*

The *majaka* consists of ringlets of bottle tops tied together with string attached around the ankles of dancers. Traditionally the bottle tops vibrators were snail or tortoise shells and of course the traditional *mupfuti* fibre is being increasingly replaced by other more easily obtained materials (see *mahlwayi*).

2.13 *Shwau*

Much smaller than the *magagada* – *magavhu* are the *shwau* leg rattles which are similar in design and worn at Chidzimba dances to appease the *shave* hunting spirits.

2.14 *Chikitsi* or *chisekesa*

Chikitsi rattle

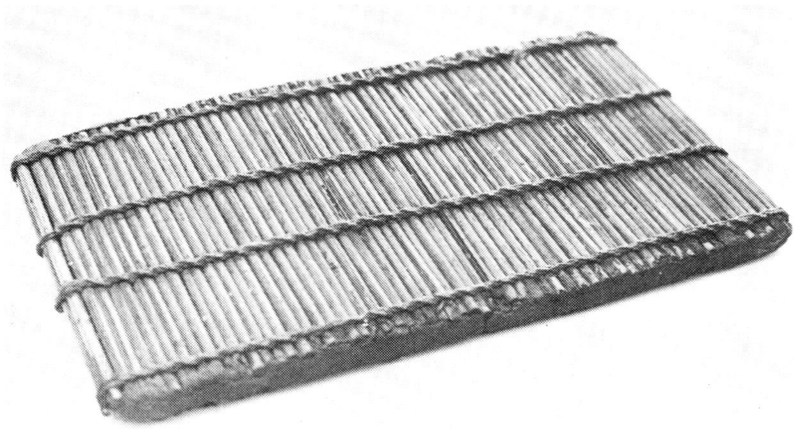

Another ideophone is the *chikitsi* or *chisekesa* which consists of two sections of interwoven reed joined together by bark fibre, sealed at the edges with clay and filled with a selection of small seeds or pebbles. This instrument is generally played by women and commonly used at wedding celebrations. It is well distributed throughout Zimbabwe, Malaŵi and Mozambique.[12] (It is derived from the smaller *mapudzi* or *shwau*.)

12 Catalogo de Instrumentos Musicais de Moçambique, Ministerio da Educação e Cultura, 1980 p.8.

2.15 Wooden clappers

The rhythmic clapping of hands accompanies many songs and dances in Zimbabwe. Different quality sound is produced by varying the formation of the hands. This basic principle is applied in the formation of yet another musical instrument known variously as *mwakwati* or *marasha* according to the region of origin. The wooden clappers, which to western eyes might be seen as resembling the Spanish castanet, are made from two hollowed out pieces of wood. Generally, a piece of wood measuring 30 cm is chosen, split in half and hollowed out. If the

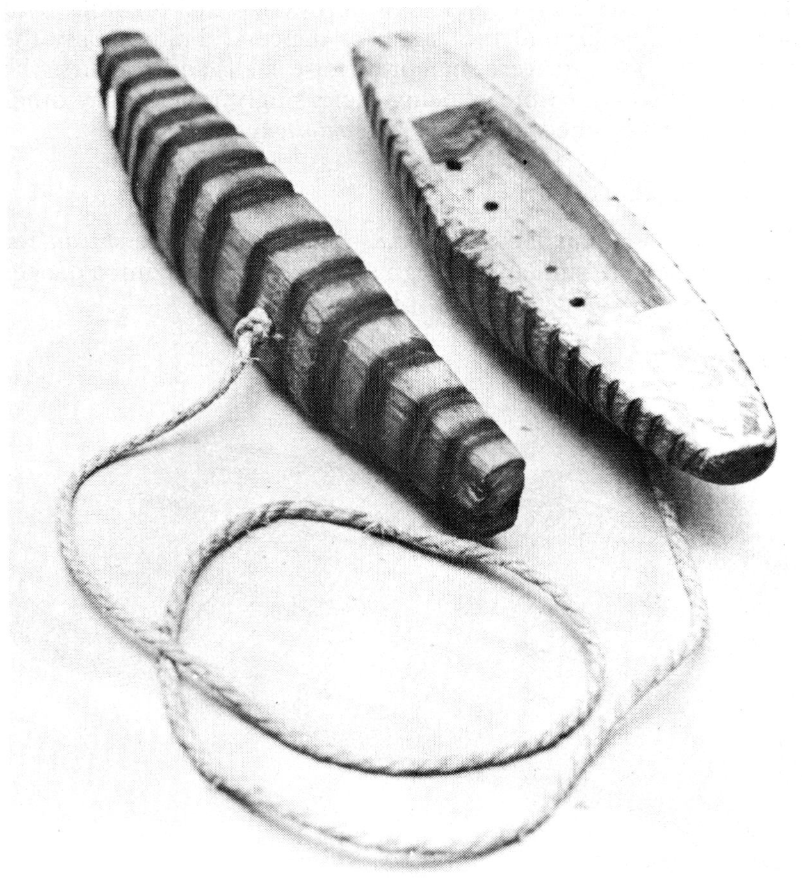

Marasha (wooden clapper)

walls are too thick, a somewhat clumsy and damp sound will emerge, whereas a clean and crisp sound will be yielded if the walls are carved thinner. The outside of this instrument may be decorated by the application of a hot iron. Very often the two sections comprising this instrument are joined by a length of bark fibre string. Clapping the finished instrument together in a parallel manner will produce bigger notes whilst clapping them together crosswise will emit the little notes. Exactly the same occurs when clapping hands.[13]

13 Bro. Kurt Huwiler, Shona Musical Instruments, 1978, Kristo.

2.16 *Matamba shells*

Neatly trimmed and halved sections of the *Matamba* fruit can also be used as clapping instruments. By choosing fruits of various sizes notes of different quality can be produced.

2.17 *Izikeyi*

Izikeyi is a very similar instrument found amongst the Ndebele people. It consists of two strong sticks which are struck together in order to create a rhythmic accompaniment for singers at traditional ceremonies. The *izikeyi* is far more commonly used by the Ndebele than drums. Wood for these sticks generally comes from the *mangwe* tree.

Magagada — made from *matamba* shells

3 Aerophones — Wind instruments

3.1 Chigufe

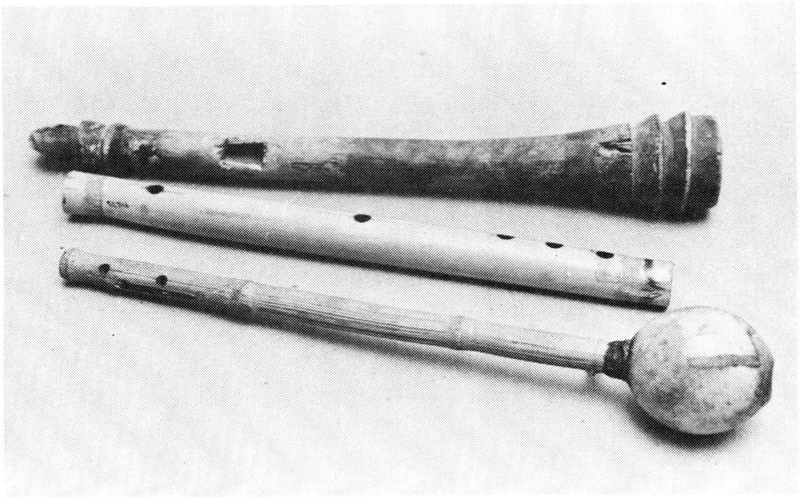

Unnamed flute type instrument from Binga, *mutoriro* flute and *chigufe*

Perhaps the best known instrument in this class is the *chigufe* which is a flute type instrument. It consists of a bottle gourd, dried *damba* or wild orange fruit of the *matamba* tree. The fruit is thoroughly cleaned of the inside pith and seeds before being well dried. A large mouth hole is drilled at the top of the shell whilst two smaller finger holes are located on the curvature of the shell. The exact position and diameter of these finger holes is most important and only experience guarantees success. The musician plays this instrument by blowing air into the mouth hole and then opening the fingerholes either full or half depending on the required tones.

3.2 Ombgwe or Humbwe

This wind instrument closely resembles the *chigufe* and is often referred to as such. It is basically the *chigufe* with the addition of a reed or cane into which a number of fingerholes are drilled. The musician blows into the *matamba* shell and varies the pitch by manipulation of his fingers over the stops. The instrument is much easier to play than the *chigufe*, which requires the player to direct the airflow over the mouth hole in order to produce a steady tone, and because this is hardly possible, it makes play a little difficult.

3.3 Modified *Chigufe*

Because of the difficulty in playing the standard *chigufe* innovative musicians have fitted a small section of reed at an approximate 45° angle so as to direct the air flow over the sharp opening of the mouth hole. The best possible angle should be determined whilst the glue holding the mouth piece is still wet. Yet another difference is the addition of two more fingerholes thus yielding a total of five notes.

3.4 *Mutoriro*

Another member of the aerophone group is the *mutoriro* flute which is made from a piece of cane or hollow wood sealed at both ends. The flutist blows into the hole at one end and by finger stops produces his characteristic sound. The instrument is very common in the south east of Zimbabwe but has spread to the Manicaland and central provinces as well. Traditionally, it was used by shepherds to accompany them in their hours of solitude.

3.5 *Kanyenge or kanyonje*

The *kanyonje* is yet another flute of the aerophone class with the base at one end and the double at the other. It is fashioned from a piece of *tsanga* reed which is hollowed out between the stops, these being called *mongo* (collectively). The instrument is normally about 25 cm in length and the fingering holes are burned out with hot irons. The base consists of one mouth hole and four fingering stops and the treble likewise. Should the notes not be true, the instrument is filled with water and shaken dry. After the water has run out the notes should be clearer and more mellow. The Kanyenge flute was often played in the Murewa and Chipinge areas. There are two different types of *kanyenge*. The first type had eight fingering holes and the second type can be described as a single flute or fife, made of similar reed, with one mouth hole and four finger stops. Furthermore it is somewhat smaller, only 15 cm in length, and hollow with natural plugs at either end. Yet another flute instrument encountered in Zimbabwe is the *rembaremba* flute believed to be an import from the Awemba of Zambia.[14]

14 O. Axelson, Notes on African musical Instruments, Art Zimbabwe, 1982

3.6 *Mikwati ye nyere*

Mikwati ye nyere or *mitwatiyenyere* is a wind instrument which corresponds to Western pan pipes. These pipes are made up of between four and fourteen pieces of reed, of varying lengths, designed to give different sounds. The pipes are threaded together by palm or tree bark fibre and tied against a V shaped wooden framework. The top node is cut away whilst the end node is left intact or sealed. The term *nyere* actually applies to the single pipe and when three or four are joined they become known as *ngororombe* which is also the name of a particular dance which

Mikwati wenyere (panpipes)

is performed for the ancestoral spirits in the Mutoko and Mary Mount region of N.E. Zimbabwe.[15]

15 O. Axelsson.

3.7 *Pembe*

Once the number of joined *nyere* or pipes number thirteen to fourteen, the instrument is known as *pembe*[15a] or sometimes as *mikwati ye nyere* and although there is much evidence that this instrument was very popular in Zimbabwe during pre-colonial times and the early part of this century it appears endangered.

15a Bro. Kurt Huwiler Musical Instruments of the Shona, Mambo, 1978

3.8 *Chiporiwa*

A very simple yet effective mouth whistle is known in Shona as the *chiporiwa*. It is formed by cupping the two hands around the chin and by positioning the thumb and index finger so that a ridge is formed just below the lower lip. The air stream is directed over this ridge and by opening one or two fingers different notes emerge.[16]

16 Ibid

3.9 *Hwamanda*

Largest of the wind instruments in Zimbabwe is the *hwamanda* trumpet made from the horn of a large antelope, normally the kudu bull. A small opening is cut into the narrow end of the horn through which the trumpeter blows, holding the horn with both hands.

Hwamanda or kudu horn

The *hwamanda* is common throughout Zimbabwe and is often used for communication, summoning people to an important event. It can be used at dances and its versatility extends to the hunt when it is blown in order to give courage to the huntsmen and the dogs. On the day of Zimbabwe's national independence, April the 18th, 1980, the *hwamanda* was sounded in order to herald this most important historic event.

A smaller version of the *hwamanda* is found amongst the vaTonga. This is made from the short horns of lesser antelopes. Similar small horns are used elsewhere in the country and their particularly mournful sound is characteristic of funerals. Such horns are often decorated with copper or brass wire work. Frei João dos Santos, writing in his diaries of 1586, noted that people used the horns of large wild animals which they called *mharapara* and therefore instruments are called *mharapara*. In modern day Mozambique, this instrument corresponds to the *mbalapala lipala-panda* or *mpundu* which is often the normal kudu horn.[17]

17 Tempo, No. 535, 11 January, 1981, Moçambique.

3.10 Nyanga – flutes (aerophones in Mozambique)

Whereas the pan pipes are nowadays very rare in Zimbabwe, they are popular and widely distributed in Mozambique where the *nyanga* flutes predominate. The flutes are made from reeds joined together in series of four to seven according to the various regions. So popular is this instrument that many names have evolved for it. The average length of the pipes varies from 24 cm to 34,5 cm with the largest being known as the *pakila grande* (literally large Pakila). Dancers accompany themselves on the *nyanga*.[18] *Nyanga* is the general name, and some of its variations are pictured (i.e. the Pakila grande and the Kalombo pequeno) (large Pakila and small Kalombo).

18 Domingo, 18.4.82, Maputo Sunday Newspaper. Article on Moc. musical Instruments.

3.11 Tsudi

Whilst the *nyanga* pipes are the most widely distributed wind instruments in Mozambique there are a number of others whose nature confirm cultural links between the people of Mozambique and Zimbabwe. The most important of these other wind instruments are the *mutoriro*, the *ipivi* and the *tsundi* flutes. All of these simple flutes occur in Zimbabwe. The *chirupe* or *chigufe* corresponds exactly to the well known Zimbabwean instrument which has a dry *matamba* fruit at one end of a hollow cane pierced by a number of air holes. Other lesser known instruments are made from antelope horns and played at funerals and ceremonies to summon ancestoral spirits. Larger antelope horns, like the kudu are used as trumpets to communicate between villages. In Mozambique, a special dance known as the *mpalassa* has evolved, where the dancers, principally elderly men, dance to the music of about eight or nine horns.

Flutes from Nyanga area

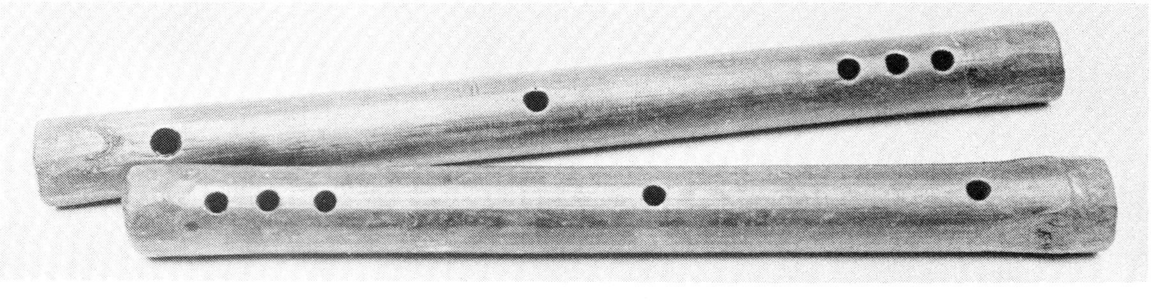

4 Membranophones — drums

The widespread Zimbabwean drum has been common for centuries. The earliest written evidence of this instrument comes from the diaries of Frei João dos Santos, who, whilst among the 'Mocaranga' (sic) noted:

> '. . . they make use of many drums, some large and some small, which they temper so that some have a treble sound and others yield other tones, and to these, those who play upon them sing with voices so loud that the whole countryside surrounding is stunned by the noise of their singing and playing.'[19]

The drum is a central part of the social and religious life of Zimbabwe where it is used at any gathering.

19 Santos João de, Ethiopia Oriental (Evora 1609) Lisbon 1892).

4.1 Ngoma

The *ngoma* is found throughout Zimbabwe in various shapes and sizes. The most common is the cylindrical type open and narrower at the bottom than at the top. The top is covered with a skin secured by wooden pegs usually made from the *chizhuzhu* tree, *(Maytenus senegalensis)*. On the highveld plateau of Zimbabwe, this *ngoma* is generally made from the *mutiti* tree *(Erythrina abyssinica)* also known as the lucky bean tree. The wood is soft and greyish and is also used to manufacture stools, toys, and mortars *(duri)*. The *ngoma* or *mutumba* are often played in a group of five drums. Whereas cow hide serves as the top skin covering for modern drums, zebra skin was once considered the absolute best with the possible exception of the skin of the riverine leguan *(bugwa)*.

Drum with opening

Another variety of *ngoma* has a number of openings cut into the cylindrical barrel of the drum. The bottom end tapers into a round point. This drum is either held between the knees of the drummer or held by the children while being played.

4.2 Chikandira

Another type of drum, again made of wood is semi-circular, with a skin stretched over the opening and secured by wooden pegs. This type is known as *chikandira* (pl). The *gandira* (s) drum which is tambourine-like is best made from the pliable *mushamba* tree *(Lannea discolor)* which is common in the woodlands of the central highveld. As the manufacture of the *chikandira* was the work of skilled craftsmen, it is nowadays very rare to find this instrument made of wood. Sheet metal is commonly used instead.

Collection of drums

4.3 Mandanda – ngoma pakatipehuru

Another type of drum similar to the *chikandira* has supporting arms on either side as handles. Otherwise the instrument is virtually identical but is known as the *mandanda* or *ngoma pakatipehuru* or *nhunduro*.

4.4 *Mutandarikwa*

Mutandarikwa — very tall drum commonly found in Masvingo province amongst the Karanga people

The extremely tall drum of almost equal circumference at either end is known as the *mutandarikwa*. It can be found amongst the chiKaranga people of Masvingo province.

4.5 *Shangani drum*

The Shangani of S.E. Zimbabwe play a cylindrical drum which is covered with a skin at both ends. The drum is suspended around the player's neck by leather straps. This instrument was used on the march during military operations and probably originates with the Nguni. The skins are laced together across the body of the drum.

4.6 Friction drum

Friction drum

The friction drum is not common in Zimbabwe. The player uses a piece of reed or stick to vibrate the top skin. The stick is held inside the drum and moved to make the required sound. The player sings to the accompaniment of the instrument.

4.7 Modern developments

Large 200 l oil drums are now used as musical instruments after covering the ends with cow hide. Such drums are common amongst the Venda people of the northern Transvaal.

4.8 *General*

Before a performance, a good drummer will carefully treat the skins with beeswax, test them for resonance and adjust the top by holding the open end over a fire to tighten the skin. Such preparation is most important if the best tone is to be obtained.

Many drums are richly decorated with carvings but regrettably this is a disappearing art. The *ngoma* is perhaps the most popular of Zimbabwean musical instruments and is played at most festivals and ceremonies. Drums will be heard with *hosho, majaka*, *magagada* and *magavhu*.

Tonga drum with elephant skin membrane, decorative carving and bark fibre rope

5 Chrodophones or string instruments

Instruments using one or more strings to produce music can be divided into three main groups, bows, zithers and lyres. Years ago, there was a rich variety of these instruments in Zimbabwe, but due to the influence of western music, the skills of playing and manufacturing of these stringed instruments have disappeared and been forgotten.[20] These instruments are extremely rare today and are usually found in the most remote rural areas.

20 O. Axelsson, Notes on African musical instruments, Art Zimbabwe, 1982.

5.1 *Chipendane*

The most common chrodophone is the bow and of these, the *chipendane* is perhaps the best known. It consists of three components, the wooden bow itself which has cylindrical sections in the middle, the string attached at either end and a small wooden stock or rod. In playing the *chipendane*, the player grasps the middle cylinder firmly with his teeth thereby allowing his mouth to resonate. The small wooden stick is then rubbed up and down the string in order to produce the desired sound. The *chipendane* was common throughout the country and traditionally was played as an accompaniment on long foot journeys.

5.2 *Chitende or ichacho*

A youngster displaying the *chitende*, an instrument often played by boys herding cattle

The *chitende* is another single string bow instrument. It varies in length with the maximum being about 2 m. The two ends are joined by a single string. Midway, the string is pulled towards the bow and tied to a bottle gourd which is the resonator. The opening of the gourd faces away from the bow.

In order to play the *chitende* or *ichacho*, the bottle gourd is held against the chest while hands grasp the bow and pluck the string. Most often the *chitende* is accompanied by the voice of the musician. This instrument is known as the *katimbwa* or *kalumbu* in some regions of Zimbabwe.

5.3 *Chidangari or kambuko*

A third variation of the bow instrument can be found amongst the vaKorekore of north-eastern Zimbabwe, particularly in the Mzarabani and Dande areas. It is less common in Zimbabwe than in Mozambique where it is found right down to the Sofala coastal areas. The instrument consists of a bow made from a riverine reed tied end to end with bark of sisal fibres although this has now been replaced by fishing nylon. At one end, there is a small piece of bottle gourd or tin sheet and snail shell vibrators. The opposite end of the instrument is held in the musician's teeth so that his mouth resonates. The string is then plucked and played to the accompaniment of a choral group. This instrument is known as the *chidangari* or *kambuko*.[21]

21 Min. da Educacão e Cultura, Moc. Catalogo de instrumentos musicals 1981, p. 22.

5.4 *Chitambe or chizambe*

The *chitambe* or *chizambe* is a bow on which the sound is produced by rubbing a small wooden rod up and down notches carved on the bow itself. The sound is augmented by the two rattles tied to the shaft of the rod. The player holds his mouth alongside the string and the mouth acts as the resonator. Most often the string is taken from *murara* palm fronds along the Sabi River. This is another shepherd's instrument.

The *chizambe* is played by some n'angas resident near Great Zimbabwe and is also popular amongst people of the Sabi river.

5.5 *Nkangala*

A very simple reed bow held together with a piece of bark fibre is known in some regions of the south-east as the *nkangala*. Together with the *chizambe* they are the only two friction bows known in Zimbabwe. The *nkangala* was traditionally only played by women and girls on returning home from the fields or during their leisure hours as the accompaniment to songs. One is held fast by the teeth so the mouth again acts as resonator and the sound is produced by the friction of a piece of broad leaf across the string.

5.6 *Venda earth-bow*

An unusual type of chordophone described as an earth-bow has been observed by Olaf Axelsson in the south-eastern corner of Zimbabwe, amongst Venda school children. To build this instrument, a pit is dug in the ground over which a metal sheet is placed weighed down by stones at the edges. In the middle of this sheet a wire, or a sinew, is tightened and stretched upwards and fastened to a springy branch which is bent over the covered pit. By loosening and tightening the tension of the branch, the wire is also loosened and tighted and thus produces a few different diatonic pitches whilst the hole in the sheet metal allows sound to escape from the resonating chamber below.[22]

22 O. Axelsson 1981, p. 12.

5.7 *Joro*

According to Olaf Axelsson of the Kwanongoma College of Music, the Shona people were once skilled at making and playing a one-stringed fiddle called *joro,* but unfortunately this instrument is now almost extinct. It consisted of a long, narrow, hollowed out stick with a resonator, usually a small metal tin fastened at the end. A string attached to the resonator was stretched along the groove and secured to a peg at the other end. The *joro* was bowed in playing.[23]

23 Ibid

5.8 *Chikwizo*

The *chikwizo* (rasping or scraping instrument) falls into the cordophone class of musical instruments. It is a very rare and unusual instrument nowadays confined to the Sabi river valley and some isolated regions of Manicaland. A good variety of mixed sound is produced by this instrument during play. The *chikwizo* is made up of three separate parts and these are described as follows:

a) The board which is made from selected timber carved into a plank with a hole in the middle. (A calabash is held beneath the hole during play.)

b) The bow, which is fashioned from a flexible tree branch which has been soaked in water for about one week in order to make it more pliant. This branch is neatly bent into the shape of a semi-circle and fitted into either end of the piece of wood or base board. Once positioned, the bow is left to harden before being carved into a series of notches from one end to the other.[24]

c) The final component part is the stick which is made from a piece of cane or reed measuring 12 to 15 mm in diameter.

The instrument is played like the Chizambe; that is by rubbing the stick up and down the notches on the bow. The vibrations thus produced resonate through the bottle gourd held underneath the instrument.

24 Bro. Kurt Huwiler, in Musical Instruments of the Shona in Zimbabwe, Kristo, 1978, Part 1 Mambo Press, Gweru.

5.9 *Mujejeje – Stonebells*

Brother Kurt Huwiler who spent many years in Zimbabwe was fortunate enough to learn of this most unusual musical instrument which is the largest ever played by the Shona in Zimbabwe. Known in the Gokomere region of Masvingo province as the *mujejeje* (stonebells or rock gong), this very unusual phenomenon is created by nature through the process of exfoliation of granite rock slabs. Granite kopjes or hills abound in various parts of Zimbabwe and in many of these, natural stonebells were adapted by the Shona of pre-colonial Zimbabwe.[25] Venturing into rock kopjes, one may well come across such rock-slabs which when struck will ring out. Proof that such well positioned rock slabs were once used as bells or gongs can be found in a series of shallow depressions along the edge. Deeper notes are produced when the rock slab is struck in the middle and higher notes will be produced when struck nearer the edge.[26]

Evidence of this unique musical tradition came to light through research of early missionary records from around the turn of the century, in Zimbabwe. When the first Christian baptism was scheduled by missionaries at Gokomere, the *vakuru* or village elders requested that the ceremony take place at a place of some special significance near Muzondo in the region of Musombo and Chiramba. The religious procession followed a winding path through the thick bush leading up to a large clearing surrounded on all sides by large rocks and stones. The clearing opened to the east and the west affording participants a magnificent panorama. Not only was the setting perfect for such an occasion but the missionaries were further rewarded by the ringing of the traditional rockbells. Singing, dancing and feasting completed a very memorable day. Anxious to recreate the haunting sounds of the rock gongs, endeavours were made to move some of them nearer to the Mission station. Such attempts failed because the stones were simply too heavy.[27] However for those willing to make the journey through the bush to listen to the unique sounds of the *mujejeje* there is a rich reward, both in the audible experience itself and the knowledge that they have participated in a very old Zimbabwean musical tradition.

25 Ibid

26 Ibid

27 Ibid

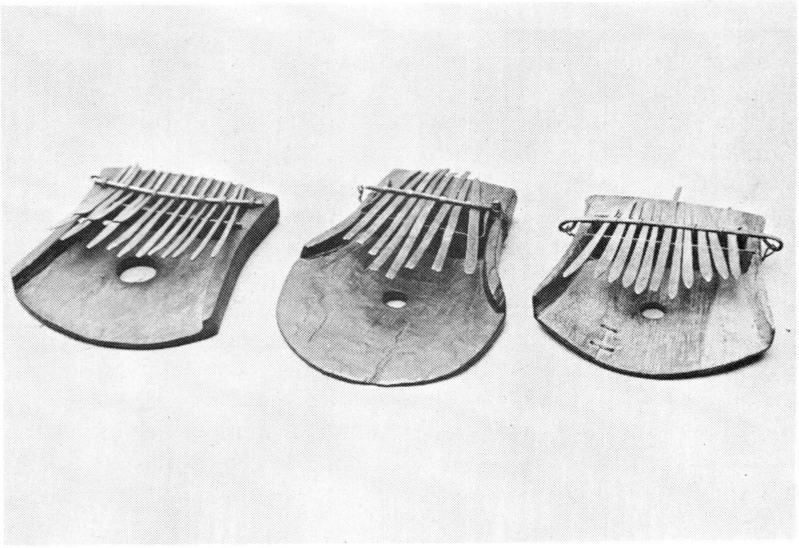

*Mbira dzava*Tonga

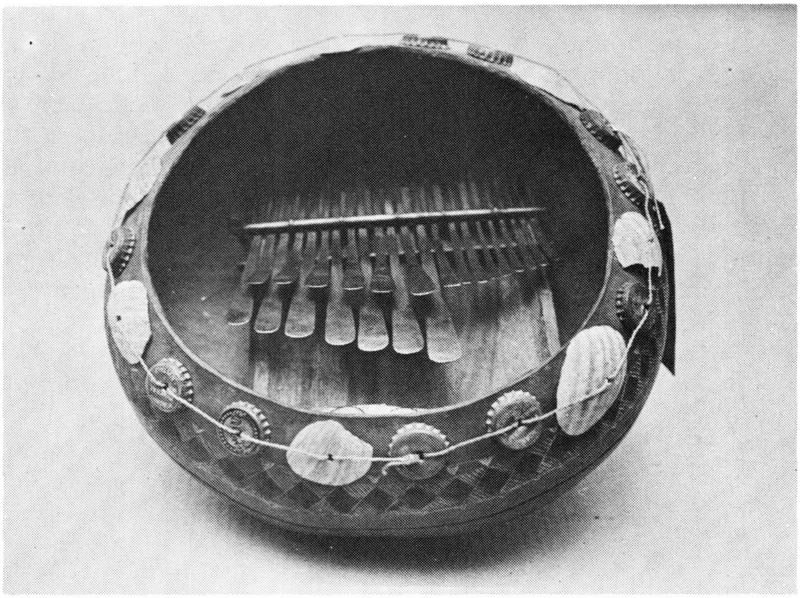

Mbira dzaVadzimu in dende calabash. The rim has been decorated with bottle tops and snail shells.

6 Pre-colonial textiles

1 Cotton weaving technology

The spinning and weaving of cotton cloth was already being practised in Zimbabwe in the 13th century and possibly earlier than that. Because the climate on the highveld plateau was cool, clothing was necessary and the Shona had developed an excellent but somewhat laborious spinning and weaving technique. Archaeological excavations of the Great Zimbabwe have revealed hundreds of discs cut from pot sherds that were used as spinning weights. These are the only remains of a considerable textile industry which once flourished at Great Zimbabwe.[1]

The wooden looms and cotton fabrics themselves have long since decayed and disappeared. Some of the cotton used in this industry was probably grown in the Zambezi valley.

Cloth was imported to Zimbabwe by Muslim traders who bought fabrics in India. Later, Portuguese traders brought in further supplies of cloth. This was not sufficient to satisfy

1 P. Garlake, Great Zimbabwe, 1982, pp. 15-16 Zimbabwe Pub. House.

Illustration of weavers working on the low wooden looms

demand and the local textile industry, based on wild cotton plants, continued up until as late as 1940. The decline of this Iron age technology was inevitable in the face of modern imports.

A number of isolated observations of the traditional spinning and weaving of cotton were made in the Mount Darwin district (Fura) in 1926 and again in 1940.[2] There is no evidence that this weaving is practised nowadays and so it is very important to record exactly how it was done in the past.

Wild cotton was gathered from plants growing in the woodlands around settlements. There seems to have been no serious attempt to cultivate the crop. Some of this fibre was red in colour.[3] Having collected and cleaned the cotton bolls, the lint was placed in a small gourd *(dembe)* from which it was spun onto a spindle *(chivhinga)*.

Amongst the vaZezuru, the process of spinning and weaving cotton is known as *kuita shinda* and the vaKorekore call it *kuita tsaru*. Spinning and weaving sometimes took place during *nhimbe* ceremonies when many people gathered together. This work was done exclusively by men who would also operate the low looms after spinning the yarn from the raw cotton boll.[4]

2 E. J. B. McAdams and R. Howman, Nada, 1940, pp. 96-100.

3 M. P. Musonza, Oral History (born c. 1886), National Archives.

4 Ibid

2 Method

The raw cotton boll was thoroughly cleaned, removing all twigs and other matter. The spindle *(hamba)* or *(chizingo)* was made from the *mugoho* or *mukombego* tree, which is very heavy and

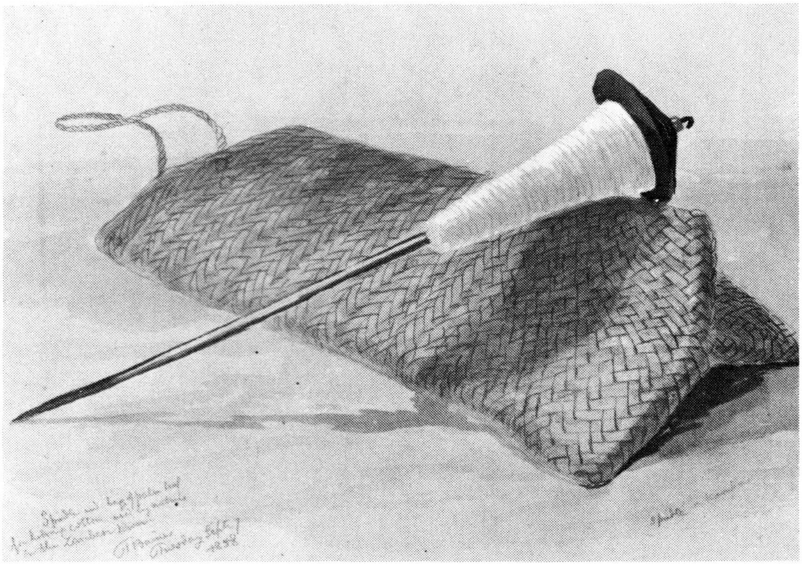

A cotton spindle and a small bag made from palm leaf

hard. The spindle measured an average 280 mm by 10 mm in diameter. At one end of the spindle a circular piece of wood some 70 mm in diameter was fitted as the spindle whorl or weights (in the case of Great Zimbabwe they used discs cut from pot sherds), which helped the rapid rotation of the spindle. A small metal hook *(karoho)* caught the raw cotton lint contained in the gourd. The spindle was made to rotate between the thumb and palm of the right hand and thus the thread was drawn out of the rough lint and onto the spindle.[5]

Spun cotton yarn was then woven on a loom as pictured in the illustrations. In June 1924 a villager was photographed weaving a large blanket on the ground loom. In 1949, the same technique was observed, although on a smaller scale. Apart from the cotton textile industry, there was another fibre, from the Mutowa tree *(Diplorhynshus condylocarpon)*. Cloth as big as modern blankets was woven either on a loom or by hand knots. This material was often known as *gupo* and was worn by women around their waist, but this method has not been recorded.[6]

5 L. J. B. McAdams and R. Howman, Nada, 1940, pp. 96-100.

6 Ibid

A complete gudza mat

3 Creative work from tree bark

The art of weaving the *gudza* blankets and *nhova* bags still flourishes in Zimbabwe. This unique and beautiful craft is practised on an increasing scale as part of a growing cottage industry in the communal sector. One particular centre of this industry is near the Birchenough bridge in the south east.

Patricia Wood, Zimbabwean artist, has observed that the *gudza* products are very fine and the work is skilled, with care being taken to ensure an even tension along the edges. Colours are introduced in shades of red, ochre, brown and black. The dyes for this are obtained from soil pigments and plant juices. Texture is sometimes introduced with patterns of knots. (These blankets are now in demand for use as wall hangings.)[7]

A Portuguese chronicler of the sixteenth century noted how the people of Batonga (Shona speaking Mutoko area) dress in the bark of trees, of which they also make containers, and which they gather in the following way:

> 'they cut the tree and hit it with sticks shaped like hammers and start stripping it and blows break the outer hardness whilst the webbing is left inside. That which they use for containers is like cork and they weave the inner bark together, namely to cover themselves (blankets) by night.'[8]

The methods of *gudza* weavers of today are similar to those described above. As imported cloths and home made *machira* were relatively difficult and expensive to obtain, most people used bark fibre cloth. Only hunters and traders could acquire skins.

7 P. Wood, Art Rhodesia 1978. National Arts Foundation.

8 Fernandez, Andre to Luis Frois, Documents, Vol. VII, Documents on the Portuguese, (25.6.1560).

3.2 Manufacture

One of the commonest methods of obtaining the bark fibre cloth was to cut away sections of tree bark from the *munhondo (Julbernadia globiflora)* or the *mupfuti (Brachystegia boehmi.)* Care was taken to ensure that the bark came away in a single piece and so only large mature trees were used. The cut section of bark was buried in the ground and the other outer layer of tough cork-like material gradually loosened using a special tool *(chikunambezo)* or *adze*. Once the tough outer material has been removed, the inner softer material is stretched out, softened and could now serve as blanket.[9]

9 Bent, Theodore, Ruined Cities of Mashonaland pp. 257-8.

4 A *Gudza* bark fibre cloth

For the more common woven *gudza*, the softer inner bark material is removed and chewed or otherwise softened and stretched into threads which could now be knotted or woven together to form the *gudza* cloth or *nhova* bags and containers. *Gudza* cloth was also used to make beer filters, filtering out sediment for which it is ideal. In some cases, the *gudza* cloth and blankets were decorated with worked designs.

Gudza and *gumbu* blankets are very warm and pliable. In the late nineteenth century, people of Gutu in the Masvingo province made use of the *gudza* cloth by weaving it into long sausage shaped casings in which they stored their provisions like dried locusts, caterpillars and sweet potatoes. These bundles were suspended from tall trees at the approaches to villages.[10]

10 Ibid, pp. 309-310.

During the 19th century, the use of bark for the manufacture of many items was common among the Karanga of Masvingo province. Bark collecting occurred at a particular time of year, and whole families would take part making the event a social occasion, when large quantities of the material were collected to make blankets and cloth, string and arrow quivers and beehives and granaries. At the same time, caterpillars and such food were gathered for storage and later consumption in winter months.[11]

11 Ibid, p. 320.

The bark fibre was woven into special garments for young women. This garment, roughly half the size of a modern day kitchen apron had geometric patterns worked into it. This textile was commonly found amongst Shona speaking people. The women of Mutoko wove massive dresses, two metres and one metre wide, which they decorated with raised geometric patterns. These were wrapped around the waist and tied with a belt of bark netting.

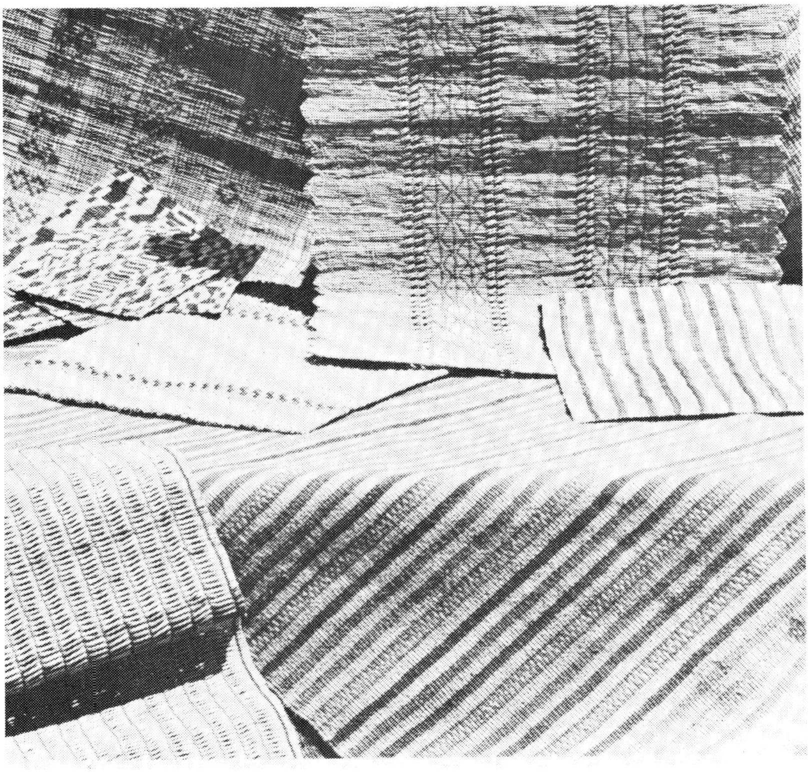

A collection of *gudza* and reed mats

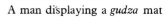

A man displaying a *gudza* mat

7 Pottery and ceramics

The history of pottery in Zimbabwe

Pottery that is used to hold grain and water, for preparation of food and brewing of beer is a symbol of the closeness of the people to the land. It is also an essential part of Zimbabwe's material culture which dates back several millennia. This chapter examines the old and the new and the combination of art and technology in this important craft.

The pottery in modern use in rural Zimbabwe can be traced back through the various traditions discovered through archaeological excavations in Zimbabwe. Basic concepts of style and design can be followed through the centuries from the stamped ware of c. 300, the Gokomere, the Harare, Musengezi, Mapungubwe, Zimbabwe and Khami traditions through into the Portuguese period and the most recent so-called Refuge period of the late 19th century which corresponds with the beginning of the colonial era. Archaeologists are able to identify people by finds of pottery which show the distinctive decorations of particular cultures. Variations of these designs — be they dentate stamps, incisions, cross hatchings, herringbone, nicks, chevrons — occur right through, and lend a distinctive character to Zimbabwean earthenware. The decorative qualities appear to

Rozwi pots

have declined with the advent of colonialism and the introduction of mass produced durable containers and vessels of all types. Although this traditional craft, handed down from mother to daughter for generations, is still practised, the fine quality of the past is disappearing. Decoration as of the old craft, has been largely superceded by some chevron decorations applied with modern paints. Nonetheless, many individual potters still do produce some very fine pieces but there certainly is good reason to revive the traditional values of the potter's craft.

2 Manufacture of pots

Traditionally, pottery is practised only by women. The clay *(ivhu re hari)* is collected from specific layers which occur in the sub soils. Such areas are usually found when exposed by river systems. Other deposits are found near ant hills. According to legend, only women beyond menopause may collect this raw clay. The belief apparently stems from the taboo which some ancestral spirits have placed upon blood and milk. Hence menstruating females were not allowed to touch the clay.

The dry clay must now be ground into a fine powder. This is normally done on a flat grinding stone *(guyo)*. Thereafter the powdered dust is sifted and winnowed to remove any pieces of grit or other impurities. The *rutsero* or *cinga* basket (winnowing basket) is used for this purpose. The clay powder left behind is now mixed with a little water and made into the ready potter's clay.

A circular platform, nowadays often a piece of flat tin, is used as a base for the pot which is built up in a series of coils. A wooden shaping tool *(mubuzo)* is used to help shape the pot into the required size and form. If the vessel is to be decorated, it will be incised with a pointed object, like a bone awl, before it is dry. At one time the potter would press beads into the neck or the shoulder of the pot as decorative indentations. Ground graphite powder *(chidziro)* is moistened and applied with the finger tips. Such graphite markings are often applied to contrast with the red haematite in V-shaped patterns around the neck of the pot. The finished pot will now be stored in a cool dry place, a grain hut for example, for 48 hours before being given the final smoothing with a rounded river pebble *(hurungudo)*. This polishing process gives the exterior of the vessel a shiny surface. A final drying process now takes place and the pot is left in the sun for twelve hours and on the fourth day the firing takes place. Pots are placed on top of each other, mouth down in a hollow in the ground. Grass, tree bark and other combustible materials are placed around and on top of the pots. In some cases the pots are

Grinding clay into fine powder

Sifting the grit and impurities from clay powder preparatory to moulding

Moulding the fine powdered material into ready clay

Having moulded the pot and applied graphite, the exterior is smoothed by application of rounded river pebbles

arranged to that the burning ashes and charcoal actually fall into them, thereby helping distribute heat evenly.

The mound is set alight and three to four hours later, or longer, depending on the quantities involved, the ash mound is carefully examined to check that the black clay has turned brownish or red which shows that the pots are now ready for removal. While still hot, the pots must be filled with a mixture of water and maize meal or liquid cow dung. The maize releases a resin which effectively seals the inside of the pot thereby water proofing it. This final finish is often neglected with the 'tourist ware' and consequently such pots are not normally watertight. Cow dung is commonly used in the Mwenezi district. Another traditional method of firing which was considered very effective, although lengthy, was recorded in Matabeleland in the early 1940s. Dry cattle manure burns very slowly and can smoulder for days on end at high and constant temperature. This is necessary for successful firing. More often, however, firing takes only a few hours. Where poor clays have been used or those which are very sandy the pots are smeared liberally with fat and allowed to stand in the sun until it has been absorbed.

If the pot is to be decorated with the common chevron patterns, this is done at any time after cooling. Modern red and black oil or enamel paints have now replaced the more traditional graphite or plumbago and haematite or ferrous stains which were common as recently as the 1930s. Whilst red and black were available in natural stains, the availability of modern paints has led contemporary potters to experiment with other colours such as green and blue and in other cases the black and white dots simulating the guinea fowl markings, common in pots produced for the tourist markets.

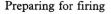

Preparing for firing

3 Pot types and function

The various pots in Zimbabwe can be roughly categorised by their shape, size and finally the decoration or its absence. The shape of the pot determines its function, size subdivides this and the presence or lack of decoration is the final distinction.[1]

1 T. Huffman, S.A. Archeological Bulletin.

Type 1 (Brewing beer) (gate or musudzi)

This type of vessel is traditionally used for the brewing of beer although nowadays 200-litre drums are replacing them. The *gate* could hold up to 50 kg of maize. This vessel is distinctive and was often used both for storing grain and brewing beer. It is made in much the same manner as the smaller pots, but the potter must stand up when making the *gate*, since she is working with so much more clay. The *gate* is generally undecorated.

Type 2 (Carrying and storing of water) (chirongo)

Chirongo — water storage vessel

The *chirongo* is used for both carrying and storing water. This pot is no longer found in urban areas because of the availability of water. In the past, young girls and elderly women carried different sized *chirongo* balanced on their heads, support provided by a grass ringlet, which was woven from *gondla* grasses. In many cases the *chirongo* was decorated with chevrons, V-shaped contrasting the graphite and haematite black and reds, and so is related to the pot described below (type 3).

Type 3 (Carrying to fields)

This type is for carrying a liquid to people who are away from their home, for instance, people working in the fields or at a wedding. The size depends on the number of people to be served, but is generally smaller than type 2 (*chirongo*), and larger

Chirongo — variation of water or beer storage vessel

than type 4 (*chipfuko*). This type has caused more conflicting opinions than any other. It appears however, that it corresponds to the more decorated *chirongo* which is often used to carry sweet, non-alcoholic *mahewu* to workers in the fields.

Type 4 (Drinking at home) (chipfuko)

This is by far the most common type and is used for beer, water and *mahewu*. Recently, the *chipfuko* has been modified by the addition of a handle. Its capacity is $^1/_2$ to 1 litre, and it has chevron patterns for decorations. Beer may be drunk direct from the *chipfuko*.

Chipfuko — mug like vessel (beer containers)

Type 5 (Baby's porridge)

Young girls will sometimes use this type to carry water because they are too inexperienced to handle larger vessels, but it is most often used for serving their porridge. Its size and shape relate it to the *chipfuko*.

Type 6 Special liquids (nyengerwo)

Nyengerwo — a beautiful and exceptional example of the potter's craft. The exterior is finely burnished and lavishly decorated. This vessel was found in the Mount Darwin district

This type can be used to contain beer or milk. It has a smaller mouth and a lid to protect the contents. Its average capacity is 20 litres. The *nyengerwo* is not common.

Type 7 Sadza cooking pot (shambakodzi)

Shambakodzi (Sh), *imbiza* (N)

Cooking pots are not generally decorated. This pot is larger than other food cooking pots because there is always more meal than meat or vegetables. More durable aluminium or iron-enamel cooking pots are replacing the *shambakodzi* in urban districts. The sides and bottom of this pot are much thicker than other pots, to sustain severe heat.

Type 8 (Sour milk)

Similar to type 7 *shambakodzi* but generally used for sour milk in the home.

Type 9 Relish cooking (chimbiya)

This is another type of cooking pot that is never decorated. It is used to prepare meat or vegetables. It is much smaller than the sadza cooking vessel because there is always less meat and vegetables than the staple maize meal.

Type 10 Relish serving vessel (hadyana)

Hadyana (Sh), *udiwo* (N)

This vessel is used to serve the meat and vegetable which accompany the sadza. The type 10 pot is nearly always decorated and is used as a serving dish.

A number of pot-types which do not fit into the above categories have been observed and these are:

Type 1a Wicker work covered (gate)

This type has been observed in the Masvingo province of Zimbabwe. The wickerwork covering is smeared with wet mud and exposed to the sun. The water evaporates, keeping the contents, water or beer cool.

Gate a very large vessel for brewing of beer, storage of fermented beer, grains, etc.

Wickerwork covered *gate* from Masvingo

Type 4a Drinking at home: (mvubelo or mbidziro)[2]

2 C. Martin, Rhodesian Scientific Association, XXXVIII, April 1941, Manyika Pottery.
C. Martin, Rhodesian Scientific Association, XXXVIII, April, 1941 p. 53 writes 'there is a big pot with two mouths called Mbidziro, used only by Chiefs and headmen on important occasions, such as the Maganza or seeding time feast. The two mouths are said to show the hospitality of the host, for two people can help themselves from it at the same time, using a gourd ladle'. Manyika pottery of the late 1930s.
(See also Harold Von Sicard. Nada, 1950)

Twin-mouthed vessel

In the Mberengwa district of Zimbabwe the multi- or two-mouthed pot is known as the *mvubelo* and according to Harold Von Sicard, in 1950, they were used for secret drinking after the public beer drinking ceremony was over. One particular mouth of the pot was reserved for the village head or chief and it was taboo for anyone else to drink from it. These multi-mouthed pots are very uncommon. The shoulders are incised with chevrons. One example is in the collection of the National Art Gallery, Harare.

Type 11 Frying pan, type (gango)

A very shallow frying pan measuring an average of 150 mm x 4 mm in depth was used to fry or roast ground nuts, maize pips or flying ants. Examples have been seen in the Zhombe region of Zimbabwe. This frying pan was more usually made from a broken pot.

Type 12 Pestle (chainga/chizenga)

This is an earthenware pestle, used to grind tobacco for snuff. The *chainga* is hand-held in grinding the tobacco in the *guyo* (stone mortar) or fragment of a large pot. It is not commonly found these days.

Type 4a Sour milk processing

Usually the *chipfuko* is used for this process. A small hole is punched in the bottom of this vessel and plugged with a porous cork which allows the whey to filter through leaving the curdled sour milk behind. The modified *chipfuko* is placed above another container.

Type 13 Zoomorphic pots

Although more ceramic sculpture than pottery, these animal shaped pots are produced wherever pottery is made. Most popular are the guinea fowl pots made for the tourist markets. In late 1900 a splendid example of Zoomorphic pottery was removed from a cave close to Great Zimbabwe. This magnificent relic resembles a zebra. It is hollow, and the head which apparently was the stopper, was missing. It measures approximately 270 mm high by 150 mm long and is marked with geometric exactness with zebra stripes all over its body. The pot is black but the stripes are a dull red colour.[3]

3 Hall and Neal, Ancient Ruins of Rhodesia, pp. 155-156.

4 Decoration

As a general rule all modern pottery used for cooking does not have any decoration. Vessels for the drinking of beer or water and those used to serve food in do. Thus the *chirongo, chipfuko, ṅyengerwo* and *hadyana* all show considerable artistic elements within established style and tradition. The decorative themes applied to the pots easily identify their cultural and social traditions. Hence the use of chevron patterns and vertical stripes which contrast graphite blacks with haematite red-ochres, and in other cases incised patterns of bands, triangles and vertical stripes, are typically Shona tradition and are immediately recognised by other Africans.[4]

T. Huffman's chart on incised decoration and colour contrasts found amongst Shona potters in Pumula illustrates contemporary decorative styles which can be traced back through the centuries. Not only are these decorative techniques easily identified with pottery of the past, but so are shapes and sizes, all of which fit into the pattern of Zimbabwean Iron Age societies as well as those of the recent agriculturalists, for until the colonial era, there has probably not been any major change in economy or technology by these Iron Age people for 2 000 years.[5]

4 T. Huffman, S.A. Archaeological Bulletin.

5 Ibid

Contemporary Shona styles

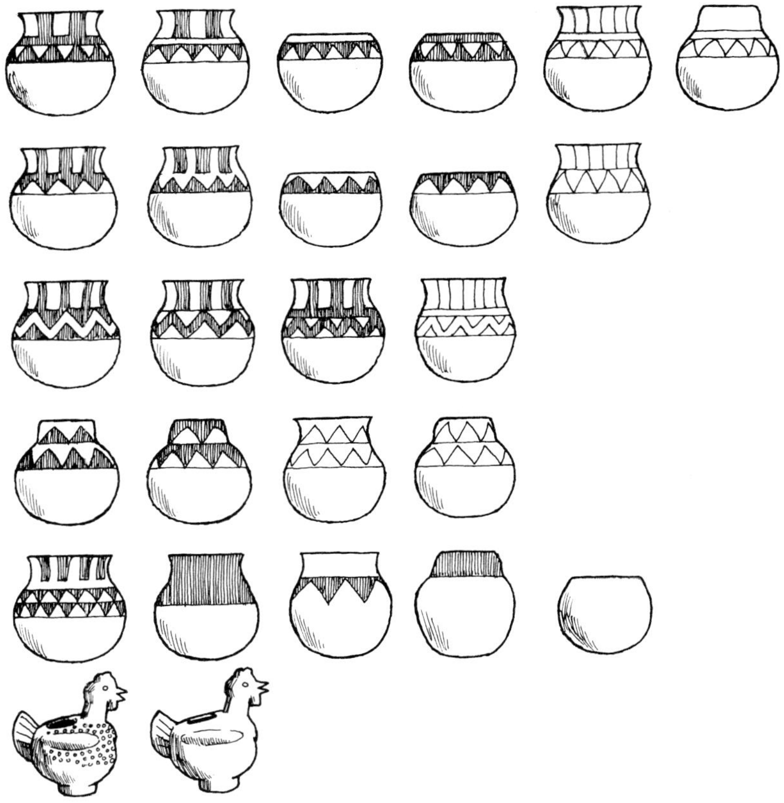

19th century Shona pottery

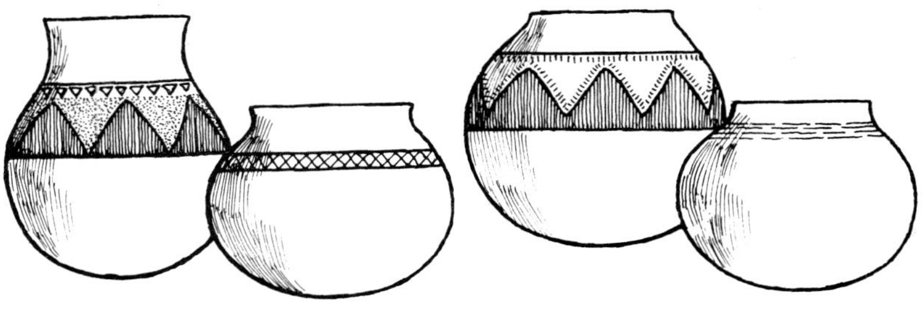

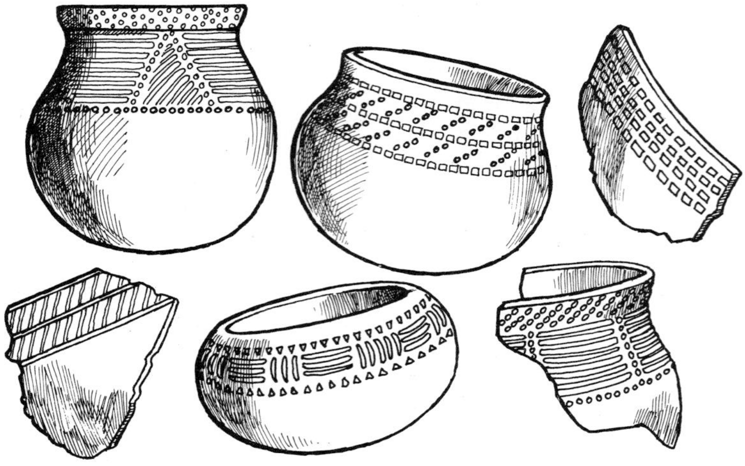

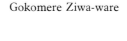

Gokomere Ziwa-ware

5 Size

The size of the pots was determined by their intended use and required capacity, which depended on many things, such as size of family, age of user, etc.

6 Chikuva — pottery display shelf

On entering a typical Shona kitchen[6] hut *(imba yekubikira)*, one sees first the raised clay dresser/display shelf *(chikuva)*, on which domestic pottery *(hari)* are arranged. The entrance was protected by a door consisting of a single wooden plank *(goni)*. Inside, a skirting board of clay *(mupfungwa)* ran around the hut edge and this was often used for seating. The skirting board and dresser were regularly smeared with cow dung and polished with green leaf pulp *(kudzura nendowe)*. Two varieties of floor mat, the *hukwe* (made from split canes strung together by bark fibres) and *nokwe* (grass or rush mat) were spread for women to sit upon whilst cooking. Suspended over the central fireplaces *(choto)* was the meat or vegetable drying basket *(mutariro)*. Hidden away in the roof rafters of the hut were kept the wooden pillows (tools and axes) *(mitsago, gano, demo, tsomo, mbezo* and *mupini)*, and the *chizenga* which is a small snuff grinder of baked clay shaped like the bowl of a large spoon. The top of the *chizenga* is perforated so it can be suspended from bark fibre string.

The *hari* on the *chikuva* would contain sour milk, beer, grain and flour. A calabash for serving water *(dende* or *mukombe)* stood next to the pots.

6 Guy Taylor, A Shona Hut, Nada, 1927.

8 Basketware and allied craftwork

1 Introduction

The manufacture of wickerware vessels from cane, osiers, reeds or rushes has been a tradition amongst the people of Zimbabwe for a long time. There are many types for many varied uses, such as grain containers or fish traps. The art of basket work has survived and flourished in Zimbabwe and various types can be seen in daily use, throughout the country.

2 Vapostori basket makers

Indeed one community, the Korsten Basket Makers who are religious followers of the Vapostori (church of God) sect, make baskets for a full time livelihood. These people, of the sect founded by Johane Masowe, who was born in 1914 at Gandanzara in the Makoni region of Zimbabwe, settled in great numbers in South Africa where they practised their trade. Fifteen years ago, the South African Government expelled the Korsten sect back to Rhodesia (Zimbabwe). Today, the basket makers can be seen along major highways.[1]

1 Munjeri, D. Korsten Basket Makers, NADA, 1978.

3 Basket types

The baskets can be divided into five main categories: *tswanda*, the *tsero*, the *chitunde*, the *duwo*, the *ingcebetu* and the *isilulu*.

3.1 Tswanda

The *tswanda* is normally a deep vessel used to store cereals and grain. This basket is generally made by men who make them from the young shoots of the *mutondo* trees. The shoots are cut into thin strips and then tied together with root fibres from the

Tswanda

same trees. The strips are woven from the base and just before the top, a section of circular *shanga* reed is introduced. The whole section is then made fast using the same *mutondo* root fibres.

3.2 Dengu

The *dengu* is similar to the *tswanda* but very much larger and is used to carry *rapoko*. This vessel was traditionally used as a measure of value in the sale of agricultural produce. The *dengu* is normally made from *chirugangu* palm and *mushamba* tree root fibres.

3.3 Tsero

Tsero (Sh), *ukhomane* (N)

The *tsero* are a class of flat open baskets used for winnowing the drying grains. The white coloured palm used in the manufacture of the *tsero* is sometimes strained with red tree gum. This serves as a preservative and seals the woven joins.

3.4 *Chitundu*

Chitundu made from grass, normally used for personal possessions. Also much favoured by n'angas or traditional healers as containers for medicines

The *chitunde* basket is a deep circular or semi-circular vessel used to store personal or medical items, used particularly among the N'anga.

Chitundu made from *ilala* palm fronds

3.5 *Duwo*

The *duwo* are the very large fish trap baskets, constructed from stout osiers woven and held fast with *mupfuti* or other tree fibres. These traps are still commonly used along the major river systems of Zimbabwe. (See traps.)

3.6 *Ingcebethu and isilulu*

Ingcebethu (N)

Ingcebethu is a class of baskets found mainly in Matabeleland and amongst the valley Tonga. (See manufacture of baskets.)

3.7 *Isitsha*

These baskets are made from *dodlane* grasses tied together in ringlets by *ilala* palm fronds. They are very common amongst the Ndebele who use them for carrying maize, pumpkins and other farm produce.

Isitsha (N): Ndebele basket used for carrying maize cobs, pumpkins and other harvest from the fields. It is made from the *dodlana* grass tied with ilala palm fronds. The grass is shaped into ringlets which are threaded together with a needle (*usunguo*). The *isitsha* basket is here pictured against the background of *icansi* mat made from *imizi* grasses

4 Mats

4.1 *Rupasa*

The *rupasa* reed mats are from *tsanga* reeds collected in marshy or swampy vleis throughout the country. The cut reeds are then dried for about seven days before being cut down the middle and then threaded together with *mupfuti* fibres. Sewing takes about two to three hours. As this is heavy work, it is generally done by men. The *rupasa, rukukwe* or *bonde* mats are made as a general purpose floor mat, sleeping mat or wall hanging for a screen.

4.2 *Nhokwe*

Nhokwe (Sh) or *amacansi* (N) mats

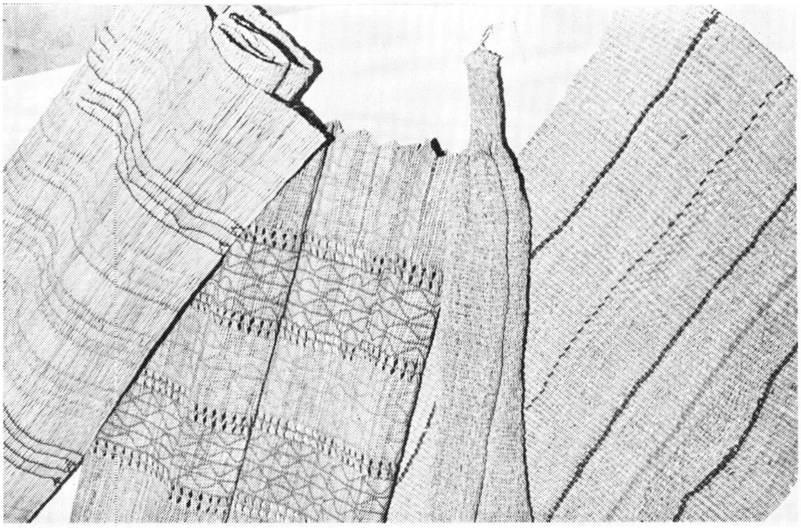

Similar to the *rupasa* are the *nhokwe* or *macansi* floor mats made from the *imizi* grasses harvested, dried and sewn together by women. The darker colouring of the *mupfuti* fibre contrasts with the light coloured grass. Not only are these mats very useful, but they are very decorative as well.

5 Manufacture of baskets

Ilala and *imizi* (palm fronds and grass) are considered the best materials for the manufacture of a whole range of baskets still in daily use in the western province (Matabeleland). These baskets range from the *ingcebethu* to the large *isilulu* in which grain is stored. During the early 1940s, an Ndebele woman called

Mazilingana made a careful record of how to go about this beautiful craft work. In those made from *ilala* (palm leaves) she recommended that the leaf be first divided into narrow strips which were then soaked in water for half an hour. The ribs of the leaves should be similarly soaked. Once sufficiently soft, a small ring is made at the end of a piece of palm leaf.

The strip is then wound in a clockwise direction, and the weaving of the basket begins. As a strip is finished, another is joined to it and when the end of the rib is reached, a grass known as *umadodlwana* is used to extend it. Care should be exercised to keep the lines of equal thickness.[2]

Having completed the bottom section of the basket, the walls are built up until the basket is completed. The size of the finished basket is determined by the intended use. Mazilingana cautioned that it was very important to keep the basket clean and neat by cutting off all frayed ends and hairs.[3]

The process for making the *imizi* reed basket is much the same except that, first of all, the sharp corners of the reed must be removed by stripping with a pin. The *imizi* reeds are sprinkled with water and kept damp until soft and workable and can be twisted into twine-like grass ropes before being allowed to dry in that form. An awl is used to pierce holes through which thread is passed, joining the coils together.[4] Patterns of dyed fronds (or reeds) can be introduced according to traditions handed down from mother to daughter. This artistic craft is gaining in popularity and there is a very high standard of basketware which could provide a large income if markets were established. The National Art Gallery of Zimbabwe placed many of these baskets on permanent display in late 1982 to promote this important art form.

2 Mhlagazanhlansi (Dr Neville Jones), My Friend Kumalo, Books of Rhodesia, 1972, pp. 100-102.
Referring to the notes of Edith Mazilingana who recorded the traditional manner in which to make baskets according to the Ndebele (1940s).

3 Ibid

4 Ibid

A type of *isitsha* basket made by women in Matabeleland.

9 Traps and hunting

1 Introduction

The need for fresh meat and animal skins for protective clothing was of greatest importance in the daily life of pre-colonial Zimbabwe. Although large numbers of cattle were kept, they were generally considered too valuable for day-to-day slaughter.

Communal hunting parties were organised from time to time but most of the fresh meat was caught in various simple yet ingenious traps, suited to a particular prey. In and around the fields near to the village, traps would be laid for field mice and other rodents attracted by the grain and other crops. Larger animals would be caught further away with traps carefully laid across established animal paths or routes leading to water. In all cases, these traps were regularly visited in order to check whether there had been any captures, and were not used on a commercial basis. Nowadays, trapping has become a notorious business with commercial poachers operating in national parks to catch elephant and rhino. The practice of setting small traps for tiny rodents such as field mice and the delicious cane rat continues and poses no real danger to the environment. With the exception of the guinea fowl and fish trap, all the traps described were recorded in the Chibi district of Zimbabwe.

2 Guinea Fowl trap

A simple and cunning device is used by rural children to catch guinea fowl — *hanga* (Sh) *ithendele* (N). Taking care to select an area frequented by these birds, a number of very deep circular holes are dug into the ground. Each hole is baited with fat maize pips or other grains. Taking cover in nearby clumps of elephant grass or bushes, the youngsters wait for the guinea fowl. Now the birds gobble up the pips and they soon stick their heads into the holes in search for more. Once the guinea fowl have stuck their heads into the holes, they are quickly seized and despatched. Carefully operated, a good number of birds can easily be trapped during an afternoon.[1]

1 W. Whacha interview, Kwekwe 1982.

3 *Chizarira* — leopard trap

Perhaps one of the largest traps devised was that designed to capture a leopard. A circular fence of poles (made from the heavy Terminalia mollis) tightly bound together with bark fibre rope is prepared. One very large pole is lifted and held in place by a trigger mechanism.

Suitable bait such as a live goat is tethered within the trap and this acts to attract the leopard by its bleating. As the leopard enters the trap enclosure, it activates the trigger and the heavy pole falls into the trap closing the exit. The top of the wooden trap enclosures is covered with logs and heavy stones to effectively prevent the trapped animal from escaping. Leopards trapped in this manner are later killed with spears and arrows fired through the fence. In the Chibi district of Zimbabwe where this type of trap was used, it is known as *chizarira*.[2]

2 Franklin H, Traps in Common Usage, Nada, No. 9. 1931, pp. 74-80.

4 Flying ant trap

Traps are not only for the capture of animals. At the beginning of the rains, termites swarm in search of new colonies. These insects, rich in protein, are considered a great delicacy in Zimbabwe, as in many other countries. The fatty insects are caught in their thousands, dried and then roasted on a pan. The easiest way to catch these insects is to construct a water trap immediately outside the ant hill exit hole. A small basin of water is sufficient to catch the winged ants as they emerge on their maiden flight for procreation. To ensure that the ants are directed to the dish of water, a grass thatched tunnel prevents them from flying away. This simple device is used to gather flying ants as a nutritious supplement to the normal diet. Soldier ants are also collected with another simple trapping device. A small piece of straw introduced into an ant hill ventilation hole is quickly attacked by the soldiers. By rapidly removing the straw many soldiers are plucked out of an ant hill and placed in a handy vessel. The abdomen of these soldiers is equally rich in protein and if one is quick enough to avoid the menacing pincers they can happily be eaten immediately.

5 *Ukuni* trap

This 'falling log' trap is still popular and can be found around vegetable gardens or along paths leading to water. It consists of a small passage through which the prey animal must pass. Moving through the confined space the animal pushes against a small net which releases the suspended log and allows it to fall down.[3]

3 Ibid

6 *Duwo* fish trap

Fish traps are made of reeds tied together so that once the fish have entered they cannot escape. The opening is so constructed to provide a narrow channel enabling the entrance of the fish but preventing exit by virtue of the jagged ends of the reeds along the opening. These traps are placed in the river at specific times of the year when fish are plentiful and moving in set directions according to breeding patterns. Often the passage is dammed and traps are placed in regular channels through which the main water flow is diverted.[4]

4 Ibid

7 Game nets *mambure*

Game nets were useful when hunting baboons[5] which were driven into them by beaters walking in extended line through the bush. Once ensnared in the nets, the animals were quickly killed. One particular method recorded consists of a long line of nets erected by means of long sticks. Once again, these nets were established along regular game trails or openings in thick bush through which the hunted animals were forced to flee from the alarming sounds of the beaters and dogs.[6]

During the time when game was still plentiful on the high plateau, specially constructed game stockades were so designed that animals would be driven into a corner by groups of men working with dogs. Once trapped, animals would be killed. Similar techniques involved for one group of hunters, remaining hidden in a half moon formation in thickly wooden country behind a kopje whilst the other group drove the game towards them.[7]

Simple game pits, consisting of deep narrow holes hidden by long grass were constructed in woodlands near to rivers. Game was driven towards such traps where they would fall and be trapped.[8]

5 Ibid

6 Bent, Theodore, Ruined Cities of Mashonaland, Books of Rhod, Reprint series 258-9.

7 Ibid, pp. 265-267.

8 Ibid, p. 55.

Traps

10 The ndoro of Zimbabwe

1 Introduction

The *ndoro* has a fascinating history within Zimbabwe's material culture and it certainly merits its own story. *Ndoro* found in Zimbabwe can be divided into two separate categories, firstly the original marine mollusc of the *Genus Conus Virgo* or the *Calcareous operculum* of large marine snails such as *Conus Turbo*,[1] and secondly the mass-produced factory copies of the natural mollusc.

1 Loveridge, J. P., Zimbabwe Science News, 16(8), 1982.

Having established themselves on the Mozambique coast and started trade links with the interior, the Portuguese learnt of the

Original *ndoro*

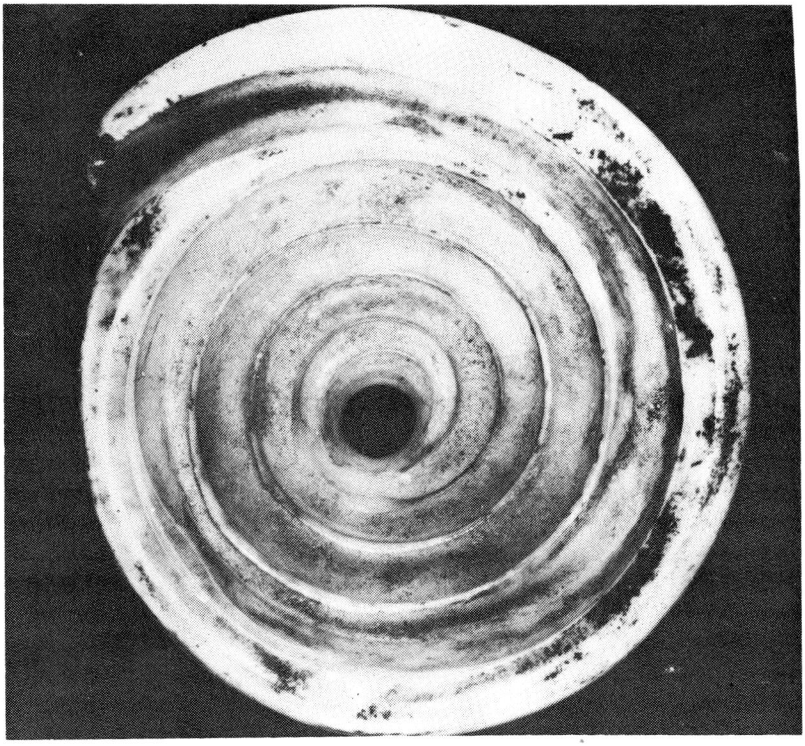

value placed upon the *ndoro*, which because of its scarcity, was much sought after. The Portuguese took advantage of this demand by introducing large quantities of the natural mollusc *ndoro* and later the mass-produced factory copies. Portuguese traders of the sixteenth, seventeenth and later centuries are believed to have exchanged *ndoro* for gold, ivory and other goods. Most of the *ndoro* found in Zimbabwe today are the ceramic or porcelain copies of the natural *ndoro*.

2 Provenance

The *ndoro* in its original or natural form consists of the bottom or flattened whorl of the *Conus Virgo* or a similar mollusc species which has been severed from the rest of the shell. *Ndoro* are heavy and of a pure white calcerous substance. The factory versions are generally of earthenware, porcelain or glassware and many of them bear serial numbers stamped on the rear. There is some speculation as to the exact place of manufacture of the ceramic *ndoro*. The most likely sources were the Portuguese in India (Goa, Damão and Diu), and possibly some came from Holland in Europe. It is most unlikely that they were made in Portugal itself.[2] All types of *ndoro* measure an average 50 mm x 36 mm thick and most of them have a central hole through the middle of the disc.

2 This is pure speculation, although it is more likely that Ndoros of the porcelain type were imported from India and Holland the exact origin has yet to be pinpointed — further research is required.

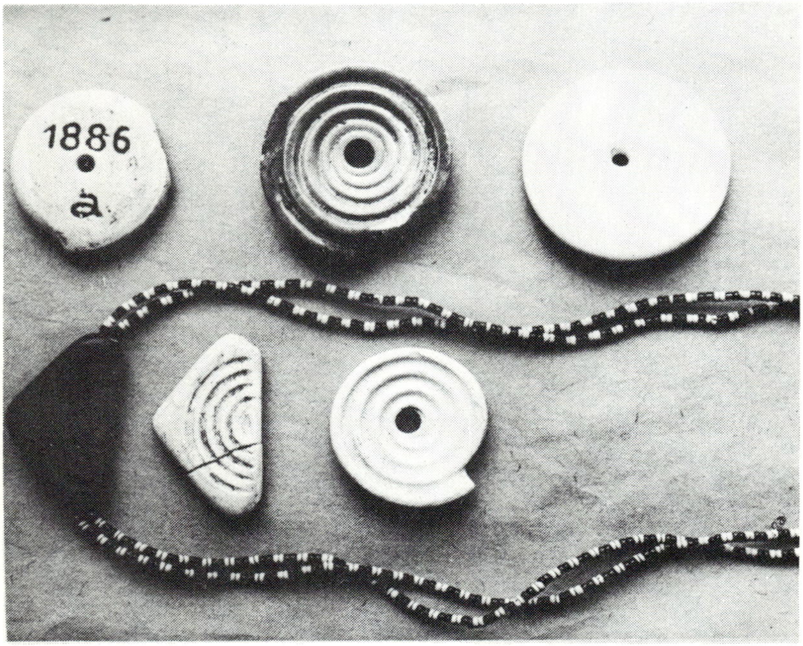

Collection of various imitation *ndoro*

3 Cowry shells

Cowry shells; *mbanyina* of the Tonga

Ndoro have often been confused with the cowry shells which are common elsewhere in sub-Saharan Africa as currency, jewellery and fertility symbols. Cowries belong to the genus of Cypraea Moneta (or Monetaria) and are about 2,5cm long.[3]

3 Loveridge, J.P., Zimbabwe Science News, 16(8), 1982.

4 Non-Zimbawean *ndoro*

In Zambia, the *ndoro* is known as the *mpande* and they are fairly common around Feira and along the Zambezi and Luangwa valleys. In southern Angola, *ndoro* are used as ornamental attachments for leather belts worn by women of the Cuanhama and Cafima region. The whole belt and ornament is known as '*ekipa*'.[4]

4 Ekipa, Angolan leather belt ensemble, using Ndoros. Details supplied by the Museu de Etnologia, Lisbon (Ref. A.H. 202.) through the kindness of Sr. Ernesto Viega de Oliveira, 1982.

5 *Ndoro* in history

Perhaps the earliest written reference to the *ndoro* can be found in the journals of a sixteenth century Portuguese chronicler who observed that:

> 'the Monomatapa and the Mocarangas and their vassals wear on their foreheads a white shell, as a jewel, strung from the hair, and the Monomatapa wears another large shell on his chest. They call these shells *andoros*.'[5]

5 Santos, João dos, Ethiopia Oriental, Cap. XVI, p. 105.

According to a colourful legend the *ndoro* played a dramatic role in our early history. At some time in the fifteenth century, it helped in a battle. The story is that a descendant of Mutota, the apparent founder of the Munhumutapa dynasty, was trying to subjugate a rival king named Karuva. Discovering through a spy that Karuva held the *ndoro* in great awe and respect, he ordered his warriors to wear *ndoro* upon their foreheads as they marched into battle against Karuva's forces. On seeing the *ndoro*-ornamented soldiers approach, Karuva became confused, and the tide of the battle turned against him.[6]

6 Oral legend supplied by A. Chigwedere during an interview in 1982. There is also the account of Karuva, the rain maker who lived near Chigango in the foothills of the Mavuradona mountains in north eastern Zimbabwe. Rivals were jealous of his attributes and eventually persuaded one of Karuva's sons, Chikuma, to betray the secret of his magic. Karuva's rivals were told to dress in various items including an 'Ndoro' which were all said to be inimical to his magical powers — magical powers which enabled him to obscure his village in dense clouds of mist when enemies approached. Discovering that the secret of his power had been sold to his adversaries, Karuva disappeared into a nearby pool where his spirit lives on (Posselt F., The Watawara and the Batonga, in Nada, Vol. 7 1929 pp. 81 and 82.)

Women weaving *ndoro*

In 1894 Alice Balfour observed,

> 'another much prized ornament you occasionally see is an ivory coloured disc, with a hole in the middle by which it is hung around the neck. The disc is about as large as the bottom of a tumbler, and with a deep spiral groove on one side, the other being quite smooth. I cannot make out whether these are natural or artificial. They are said to come from a long way off inland and it is very difficult to induce a native to part with one.'[7]

Ndoro still enjoy a fairly wide distribution throughout the country and examples of the various types can be found in the rural areas. They are of course more common in those areas influenced by the Portuguese, i.e. N. E. Zimbabwe and the Zambezi valley system. One particular series of ceramic *ndoro* very common in the Binga region is numbered 10615 on the rear and this is believed to be a batch number produced in the 19th century. Another type of *ndoro* carries the serial number 1886 (possibly a year number) with the letter a beneath. All these have been found in the Semchembwa region of N. Zimbabwe near Binga.

In the north east of Zimbabwe there is much oral history suggestion that *ndoro* were brought into the country by the *Muzungu* or *Gouveias,*[8] by which is meant Portuguese traders from Mozambique. *Ndoro* were used by Chiefs in Shona society as symbols of rank and authority. They were also used to signify wealth. This practice continued until the colonial era when the British South Africa Company (B.S.A. Company) discouraged the used of *ndoro* in favour of their own badges of authority.[9] These (B.S.A. Company) Chief's badges were half moon shaped and the first issue of 1898 bore the Company's coat of arms. This issue was later replaced by three further issues of 1907 to 1973. A final type emerged in 1982 with the Zimbabwean Government coat of arms. It was important for the B.S.A. Company and following Rhodesian administrations to destroy the Shona hierarchy and replace it with their own systems. The B.S.A. Company, in order to consolidate its power, replaced the traditional rulers and leaders with the men of their own choice. These men were given the B.S.A. Company half moon medals.

Some unusual variations of the standard *ndoro* have been found in Zimbabwe. In 1927 a disc of iron, apparently imported from Mozambique, served as an *ndoro* for Chieftains of the Chimanyika who wore the discs on their left forearm or on the forehead.[10]

Triangular shaped *ndoro,* both the traditional white and also red have been found amongst people of the Gokwe district. The only resemblance to an original *ndoro* can be found in the whorl like impression imprinted on one side. A dealer in Harare offers *ndoro* for sale at around $50,00 and some very poor plastic copies can be bought in the Harare Msika at around $2,50 each.

7 Balfour, Alice, Twelve Hundred Miles in a Wagon, 1895, pp. 215-216.

8 Gouveia, or more correctly identified as Manoel Antonio da Souza, a Goanese born Prazeiro or Prazo Holder, who roamed around the N.E. of Zimbabwe in the late 19th century trading with the Shona.

9 Interview with A. Chigwedere in early 1982.

10 Franklin H., Nada No. 5. 1927, pp. 56-60.

6 The Nyandoro people

Oral history of the Nyandoro people indicates that some time in the 18th century their ancestors migrated into the N.E. of Zimbabwe from the Tete region of Mozambique. They finally settled in the Chiota and Chinhoyi areas where many of the clan live today. Ndoro is therefore most likely the origin of the Nyandoro clan name whose *chidao* is Unendoro, i.e. You have the chiefly medal.[11]

11 Chigwedere A., From Mutapa to Rhodes, MacMillan, p. 105.

7 Medicinal and religious connotations

Ndoro and fragments of *ndoro* have been used as a form of *hakata* or divining tablets. (See p. 22.) This has been encountered in the Zhombe communal lands. A herbalist in Kwekwe uses scrapings from a genuine mollusc in a mixture of milk as a treatment for certain eye ailments. The herbalist practising this treatment says he inherited the *ndoro* from his ancestors of the Mount Darwin district.[12]

Ancestral *ndoro* are often worn by men and women possessed by *shave* (spirits). These *ndoro* are demanded by the spirit before it appears in the chosen medium. To prevent trouble for the family, *ndoro* must be kept by the rightful inheritor. *Ndoro* of an ancestor must be worn when performing the *chidzimba* dance to appease the hunting spirits.

12 Ellert, H. Zimbabwe Science News, 16 (5), 120, 1982.

8 *Mbanyina* — cowry of the valley Tonga

Amongst the vaTonga they are known as *mbanyina* and are worn joined or woven with tree bark fibre ringlets. The shell ringlets were threaded into the hair to prevent them falling off. They served as lucky charms, currency or as both and are earlier than the *ndoro* disc. Modern cultural history of the vaTonga indicates their use as marriage tokens. The groom would give a ringlet to his intended bride's aunt as a promise or pledge. The *mbanyina* cowry shell ringlets were sometimes accompanied by a ceremonial iron hoe.

To enable easy threading, the top section of the shell is removed. It is argued that this now represents the vagina, and so is symbolic of fertility. (These ringlets have virtually disappeared from modern use and the examples illustrated were specially threaded from collections still in the remote rural areas of Binga and Siabuwa.) The cowries found in Zimbabwe belong to the species Cypraea (Monetaria) Moneta and measure on average 2,5cm long. They are similar to those distributed throughout Africa, south of the Sahara.[13]

13 Loveridge J. P., Zimbabwe Science News, 16(8), 183, 1982.

11 *Pipes and smoking*

1 Introduction

In the vaTonga pipe, the smoke is filtered and cooled by passing through water in a similar manner to the middle eastern hookah. The clay tobacco holding bowl fits onto a piece of reed which is screwed into a pre-selected and suitable calabash. The reed is wedged almost to the bottom of the calabash through a small hole drilled in the water holding part of the calabash. Joints are firmly cemented with wet clay. The tobacco bowl is detachable from the reed pipe and can easily be replaced if broken.

In preparing the pipe, the calabash is filled with water to a level where it narrows into the long stem. Smoke is then drawn down the reed tube into the calabash where it bubbles up through the liquid into the stem and into the smoker's mouth.

VaTonga women smoking

2 Tobacco

What may be loosely termed a type of tobacco bulrust consisting of a mixture of slightly crushed millet, maize chaff, bulrush millet or even genuine tobacco leaves is still commonly used by the vaTonga in the above mentioned *nefuko* pipe.

3 VaTonga smoking habits

The *nefuko* is still used, almost only by women, and is said by them to be cool and fragrant. Up until independence in 1980, women of the vaTonga on reaching puberty had their four front teeth extracted from upper and lower jaws. Also, the tissue between the nostrils was pierced enabling the introduction of a *kasinga* reed of 4 to 6 cm in lenth. Smoking, which they now took up, indicated that they had come of age. Fortunately this practice has been severely discouraged.[1]

1 It was a policy of the Rhodesian Government (implemented through the Internal Affairs Ministry) to suppress the development of the Zambezi Valley Tonga into the twentieth century. The intention being to preserve the Tonga in a primitive stage of development as a tourist attraction. Thus the practices referred to were condoned.

4 *Gonamombe*

Gonamombe consists of a raised earth mound hollowed out at the top and filled with hot coals. A mixture of tobacco and *mbanje* or dagga (indigenous marijuana) was added to the coals and the smokers would sit around the mound, and insert hollow reeds through which they drew the intoxicating smoke into their lungs.[2]

This somewhat exotic habit has almost disappeared because of laws against the use of drugs. However the practice continues in isolated rural villages when elderly men may gather during the evening to enjoy the traditional *gonamombe*. This will be accompanied by much talk and merriment until the smokers become drowsy.[3]

5 *Mutoko wembanje*

In 1929, it was observed that adolescent boys in the Murewa district smoked dagga by making two inclined holes in the ground, in one of which the bowl is formed from clay, and in the other a reed is put. Water is poured down the hole and the smoke is then inhaled through the reed. This habit was, as a rule, discouraged by elders, and the young culprits severely beaten if caught.[4]

6 Soapstone pipes

Archaeological excavations and modern mining developments on the site of pre-colonial workings have yielded examples of soapstone pipes which were probably used together with a reed stem. Tobacco with dagga may well have been smoked in these pipes.

Dagga smoking pipe

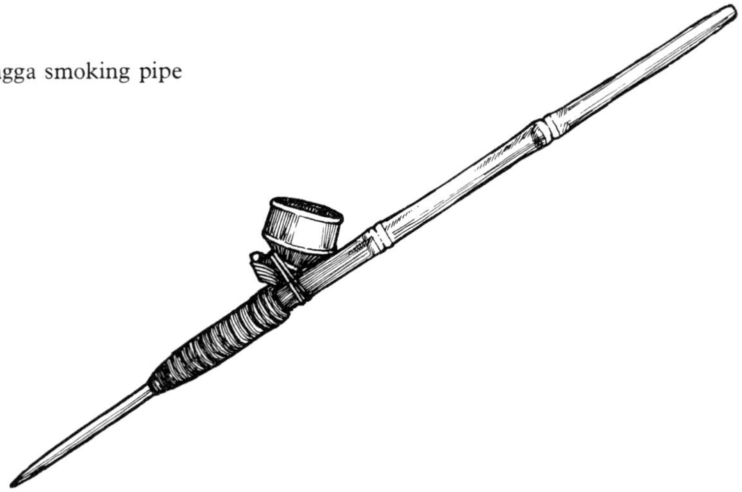

2 The smoking of dagga has long been a tradition and has never been viewed as being particularly undesirable. Dagga often took the place of alcohol in providing some relaxation from the rigours of daily toil. Thomas Baines, Explorations in S.W. Africa, Books of Rhodesia reprint edition, 1973 pp. 202-204, observed how:

> '. . . among the Fingoes, the pipe, as here, is a stone bowl inserted by its wooden stem into a horn of the proper curvature. The party sit in a circle, then No. 1 inhales the much loved vapour, passes the pipe to his neighbour, takes a mouthful of water without drinking it, passes on the calabash, and then through a tube spits out smoke and water together into a hole common to all the party . . .
> The Bechuanas make two holes in the ground, and connect them by a rather scientific mode of tunnelling. Water is then poured in, and above its surface, in one hole, is placed a little tobacco, the man kneels down, applies his mouth to the other, and enjoys the luxury of an unportable hubble-bubble.'

3 Interview with Nathaniel Chimombe, November, 1982, who reports that the smoking of dagga through the raised earth mound is still practised by some elderly people in various parts of the country.

4 Edwards, W, in Nada No. 7 1929 pp. 24-25.

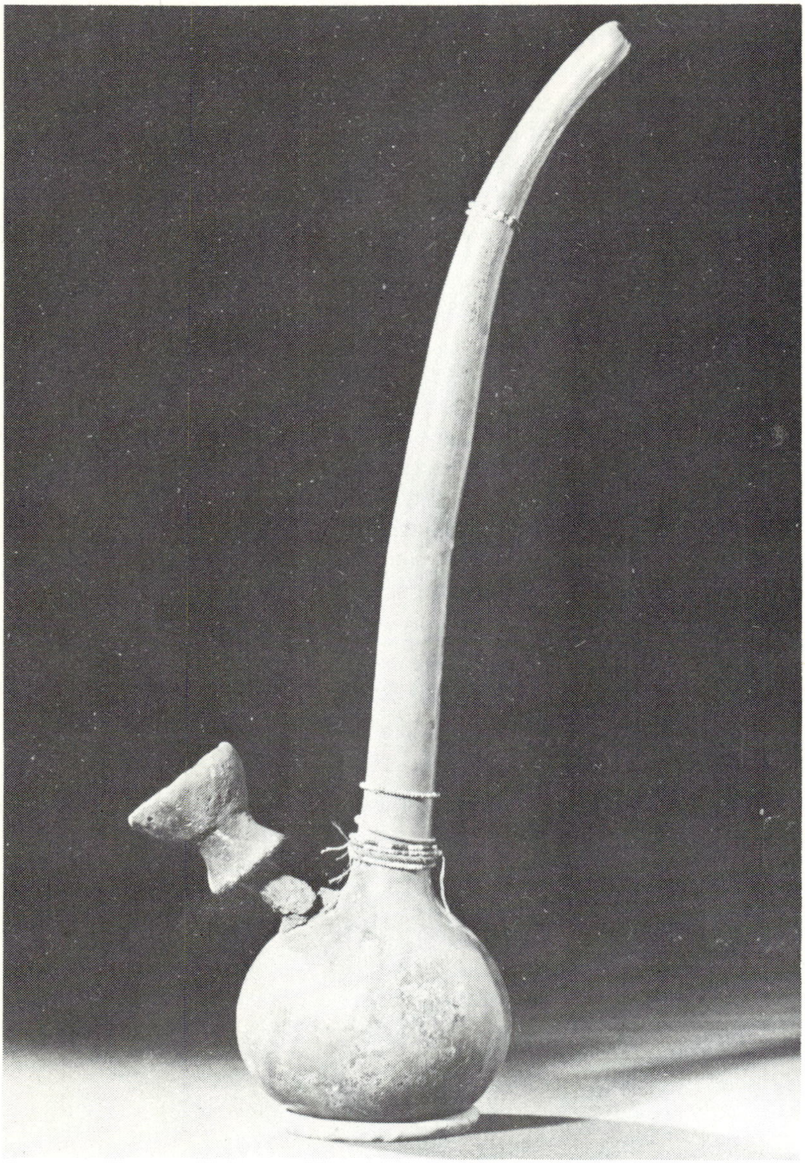

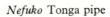

Nefuko Tonga pipe

12 Games and pastimes

The game of tsoro

The game of *tsoro* is not unique to Zimbabwe as it can be found in most central and eastern African countries including the Indian ocean islands. Essentially the game is played on a wooden board or in holes dug in the ground. Four rows of between thirteen and nineteen shaped holes *(magomba)* make up the board and two of these are allocated to each player. The game is played with a number of small stones called *matombo* or *minyira*[1] with two for each hole with the exception of the penultimate and last holes on either side of the row which have a single stone and nothing respectively. The object of the game is to move the stones anti-clockwise and according to certain rules take the opponents stones as in chequers (draughts).

1 Tracey, H. T. Rules of Tsoro, Nada, 1931 p. 33.

No doubt identical to the game of *tsoro* was that described as *fuva* which was observed at Mugabe's village of Baramazimba in the Masvingo province, during the late 1890s. The game was played by up to ten men who moved bits of pottery or stones from one hole to another in a seemingly incomprehensible manner. This favourite game of the Karanga consisted of sixty

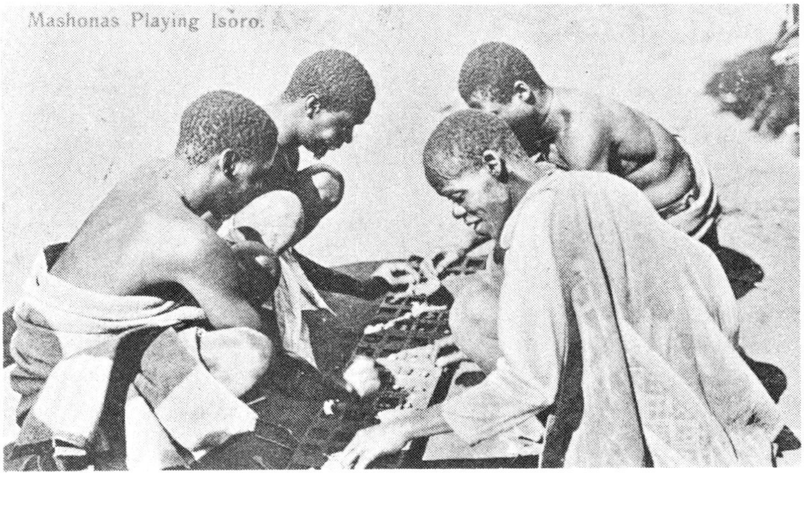
Mashonas Playing Isoro.

Men playing *tsoro*

holes in the ground arranged in four rows. In other cases, only thirty-two holes arranged in rows of four made up the game.[2]

Although *tsoro* is most often played on the ground or specially carved wooden boards, relics of soapstone *tsoro* boards have been found, which indicates that the game has been known in Zimbabwe for hundreds of years.[3]

Curiously, late nineteenth century travellers speculated that because of the vaKaranga's fondness for the game of *tsoro*, his ability to calculate was higher than that of non-*tsoro* playing kinsmen.[4] Although the game of *tsoro* is played throughout Zimbabwe whenever a group of men have the time to sit and talk in the shade of a spreading tree, no real effort has yet been made to popularise the game to the extent that it is made an official sport in the same manner as chess or bridge clubs have done. In modern day Mozambique, there is a strong move to make *tsoro* a representative sport and form national teams to play for their country. Perhaps a similar development could be considered for Zimbabwe for there must be thousands of skilled players who could play well against rival teams from neighbouring countries such as Mozambique, Zambia and Malaŵi.

2 Bent, Theodore, Ruined Cities of Mashonaland, reprint Books of Zimbabwe, pp. 85-86.

3 Hall and Neal, The Ancient Ruins of Rhodesia, reprint pp. 152-153.

4 Bent, Theodore, p. 86.

2 *Kudoda* or *nhodo*

This is a relatively easy game to play but does demand a very high degree of manual dexterity and is therefore played most often by youngsters. The players scoop out a small hollow in the ground about 10 cm in diameter. A number of small stones *(matombo)* and one large stone or tree nuts are all that is required for this game which involves throwing the stones or tree nuts into the air and catching various combinations before they fall to the ground and back into the hole. The large stone or tree nut, which is central to the game is called the *mudodo*.[5]

5 Nada, 1964.

3 Housekeeping game *(mahumbwe)*

Boys and girls, on reaching puberty, often gathered, under the supervision of adults, to play house. In the Murewa district this game, *mahumbwe*, played an essential part in preparing adolescents for their future roles in life. Makeshift huts were contructed by the boys who paired off with chosen girl friends. During the season of the game, the girls stayed at home preparing food and carrying out household chores whilst the boys went hunting with their little spears, bows and arrows. The month-long *mahumbwe* ended with a special beer being brewed by the girls. Villagers and parents of the participants attended this final ceremony at the end of the game. Not only did the *mahumbwe* serve as an amusing pastime but it also marked an important coming of age and step towards marriage.[6]

6 Hinde, C. A. Nada. No. 10, 1932 p. 99.
Edwards, W. Nada, No. 7, 1929 p. 25.

4 *Hure kure* game

This game was often played by youngsters out herding cattle. In turn, players would plant their sticks *(tsvimbo)* in the ground while their companions, a distance away, attempted to throw their own and knock the planted sticks down. If the stick is struck, it is removed to a further distance and again thrown at. If the stick is not struck, the owner removes his stick and joins the others in throwing at the next player's stick.[7]

7 Ibid, 1932 p.99.

5 The game of *ndoma*

Like hockey, this game is played by both boys and girls, and requires stamina and a cool temper. The game requires a ball, which is made out of a tabular root or spherical piece of wood. Two opposing teams faced each other on a pitch marked by boundary lines. The aim is to hit the ball *(ndoma)* into the open side and across his boundary line.[8]

8 Ibid,1932 pp. 101-102.

6 Grinding stone game *(chisiko)*

On very hot days when there was nothing much to do except shelter from the noonday sun, boys and girls often played a game of spinning *nyimo* beans into the hollow grinding stone — *guyo*. Individual beans, the more the better, are spun into the *guyo* and the object of the game is to knock out the opponents' beans. On occasions, adults came to participate and demonstrate their superior skills.[9]

9 Ibid, 1932 pp. 100-191.

7 *Chivhiri* or spinning top

This has two variations, one the cone shaped spinning top, and secondly the *matamba* shell cut in half and threaded on a *mupfuti* fibre, swung round and pulled tight.

The rules of the game *Tsoro*.

(From an original article by H. T. Tracey.)

The board consists of four rows of holes in the ground, and may be from thirteen to nineteen holes long. The game is played by two men sitting opposite each other. The object of the game is to win by out-manoeuvering the opponent, reducing him to a standstill within the rules of the game. The holes *(makomba)* are cup shaped and about 3 inches across. The stones or men *(matombo* or *minyara)* are often made from small pebbles. An advantage in the game is referred to as *baya*. The board is set by putting two men or stones in each hole, except in the two left-hand holes, which remain empty, and the hole second from the left on the front rank, in which only one stone is placed; thus (see sketch):

(2)	(2)	(2)	(2)	(2)	(2)	(2)	(2)	(2)	(2)	(2)	(2)	(2)	( )	A
(2)	(2)	(2)	(2)	(2)	(2)	(2)	(2)	(2)	(2)	(2)	(2)	(1)	( )	
( )	(1)	(2)	(2)	(2)	(2)	(2)	(2)	(2)	(2)	(2)	(2)	(2)	(2)	B
( )	(2)	(2)	(2)	(2)	(2)	(2)	(2)	(2)	(2)	(2)	(2)	(2)	(2)	

A and B, the players, move in turn in an anti-clockwise direction. Advantages can only be scored on the front rank or firing line, the back rank being the reserve line.

A point or advantage is scored when at the end of a move the last stone falls into an empty hole in your front rank and opposite an occupied hole in your opponent's front rank, when certain forfeits may be claimed. Should your stone fall into a hole opposite an unoccupied hole in his front rank, it does not score a *baya*.

Forfeits are as follows:

For the first advantage gained by both players, you may claim all the stones in the holes opposite the hole in which you scored the *baya*, plus any five holes on his board.

For the second advantage, the two opposite holes, plus any three holes.

For the third, and all subsequent advantages, the two opposite and any two holes.

The moves:

All moves are made in an anti-clockwise direction by picking up all the stones in a hole directly next in order to an empty hole (except in the first move) and by spreading them along the line, one stone in each hole. Should the last stone in your hand fall into an occupied hole, you must pick up all the stones in that hole and continue to spread them along the line until the last stone does fall into an empty hole. Whether or not this stone scores a *baya* depends upon the rules governing the advantages (see above).

The first move or opening gambit by both players is always to move the two stones out of the third hole from the left of your front rank, making a *baya* on your extreme left hole, and thus claiming the two opposite (his extreme right) holes and the five forfeits.

The board after the first movement by each player would appear as below, the five forfeits being taken with the object of hampering his movements to your advantage or to defend your vulnerable front line:

( )	( )	( )	(2)	(2)	( )	( )	(2)	(2)	(2)	(2)	(2)	(2)	( )
( )	(2)	(2)	(2)	(2)	(2)	(2)	(2)	( )	(2)	(2)	( )	(2)	(1)

(1)	(2)	( )	(2)	( )	(2)	(2)	(2)	( )	(2)	(2)	(2)	(2)	( )
( )	(2)	(2)	(2)	(2)	(2)	(2)	(2)	(2)	( )	( )	( )	(2)	( )

No single stone can move more than one hole at a time unaided by other stones or score a *baya*. Example of a move on a board set up as follows:

(3)	(2)	( )	(2)	(1)	(2)	(2)	(3)	( )	(2)
		b					a		

a move from (a) or (b) would result thus:

(3)	(2)	(1)	(3)	( )	(3)	(3)	( )	( )	( )
		b					a		

the single stone arriving at (b) would, in correct circumstances, as indicated above, constitute a *baya*. *(with acknowledgements to H. T. Tracey.)*

List of trees, bushes, grasses, etc., from which many of the tools, implements and artifacts are derived. All the species mentioned occur on the Zimbabwe highveld plateau.

Tree species	Application
Mugaragunguwo (Sh) *isafice* (N) *Ozoroa reticulata*	Used to make arrow heads, and also added to molten iron during smelting as this improved the quality of the metal, making it more malleable.
Rubber tree *mutuwa* (Sh) *inkamasane* (N) *Diplorhynchus Condylocarpon*	The latex is used in eastern Zambia to smear on the hides of drums as this improves the quality and tone.
Cabbage tree, *mufenje* (Sh) *umelemele* (N) *Cussonia Kirkii*	This timber can be used for the keys of the African Marimba or xylophone.
Large fruited combretum, *muruka* (Sh) *umbondo* (N) *Combretum Zeheri*	The roots yield a fibre which is used in making baskets and trays.
Mushava (Sh), *Inyunya* (N) *Monotes Glaber*	This timber can be used for hut rafters.
Mufuti, Mupfuti (Sh), *itshabela* (N) *Brachystegia Boehmii*	Makes excellent bark fibre rope — an all purpose bark fibre.
Mnondo, Munhondo (Sh), *umshonkwe* (N) *Julbernadia Globiflora*	Another all purpose bark fibre. The timber is used for canoes and mortars *(Duri)*.
Monkey Bread, *Mutukutu* (Sh) *Ihabahaba* (N) *Pilostigma Thonningii*	The bark contains fibre used for making string and rope.
Muriranyenze (Sh), *umnonjwana* (N) *Albiza Antunesiana*	Drums, mortars and beaters for driving fish into nets are made from this timber.
Mupangara (Sh), *ugagu* (N) *Dichrostachys Cinerea*	Tool handles can be made from this wood.
Lucky bean tree, *Mutiti* (Sh) *Umgqogqogqo* (N) *Erythrina Abyssinia*	Stools, toys, drums and pestles.
Mukwa, Mubvamaropa (Sh), *umvagazi* (N) *Pterocarpus Angolensis*	Plates, mortars, drums, canoe paddles, spear handles.
Snake bean, *Mucherekese* (Sh) *umketsheketshe* (N) *Swartzia Madagascariensis*	The black heartwood is very hard and can be used to fashion small ornaments.
Snot apple or tree hibiscus, *Mutohwe* (Sh), *Uxhakhuxhaku* (N) *Azanza Garckeana*	Sometimes used for tool handles when better woods not available.
Waterberry, *Mukute* (Sh), *imiswe* (N) *Syzygium Guineense*	Dug out canoes.
Wild pear tree, *Mutongotowa* (Sh), *Umwane* (N) *Dombeya Rotundiflora*	Bows and tool handles can be made from this timber.

Monkey orange, *Mutamba-muzhinyu* (Sh), *Umkhemeswane* (N) *Strychnos Cocculoides*	Used to make tool handles as the wood is pliable. The fruits are used in making *Hosho* or hand rattles.
Marombe or *Muenje* tree	Marimba keys are made from this wood.
Mapudzi marrow	Gouds or resonators for the Marimba, Hosho (hand rattles).
Shwawu marrow	Also used for the Hosho or magagada.
Ilala or *Murara* palm	Used for making a variety of baskets.
Chizhunzhu (Sh) *Maytenus Senegalensis*	This wood is used for the pegs which hold the skin over the drum opening.
Mushamba (Sh) Lannea discolor	Used in making of the Gandira drum.
Mukombegwe tree *Murwiti* tree	Both types are suitable material for carving headrests *(Mutsago)* in the Masvingo district.
Umangwe-omkhulu (N) *Terminalia Mollis*	Suitable wood for carving migoti or large sadza stirring spoon. This timber is very heavy indeed and therefore suitable for traps.
Uturu bush *Strophantus speciosus*	A source of poison for arrows.
Mutondo tree	Provides fibre from the roots, used in basket weaving.
imizi grass	Manufacture of some baskets and mats.

Source: Common Trees of the Highveld, D & C Palgrave, Longman, 1973.

Bibliography

Beach, D. N., *The Shona and Zimbabwe,* Mambo Press, 1980.
Balfour, Alice, *Twelve Hundred Miles in a Wagon,* Reprint, 1970.
Berliner, Paul F., *The Soul of the Mbira,* Univ. of Calif. Press, April, 1979.
Bent, Theodore, *Ruined Cities of Mashonaland,* Books of Rhod, 1969.
Catalogo de Instrumentos Musicais de Moçambique, Min. of Education and Culture. 1980. INLD.
Chigwedere, A., *From Mutapa to Rhodes,* Macmillan, 1980.
Carnegie, David, *Among the Matabele.*
Chakaipa, P., *Pfumo re ropa,* Longman, 1966.
Documents on the Portuguese, Lisbon and Harare, Vols. 1-8, NAZ.
Garlake, Peter, *Great Zimbabwe,* Zimbabwe Publishing House, 1982.
Hall, R. N. and Neal, W. G., *The Ancient Ruins of Rhod.,* Methuen, 1904.
Hemans, H. N., *The Log of a Native Commissioner,* London, Witherby, 1935.
Jones, Dr Neville, *Mhlangazanhlansi, My Friend Kumalo,* Books of Rhod., 1972.
Mutswairo, S., *Feso* (Reprint), Longman, 1982.
Mcdonald, F. W., *The Story of Mashonaland and The Missionary Pioneers,* London, Wesleyan Mission House, 1893.
Música tradicional de Moçambique, Min. da Educacãoe cultura, RPM, 1980.
Selous, F. C., *Travel and Adventure in S.E. Africa,* 1972.
Selous, F. C., *Hunters Wanderings.*
Reynolds, B., *The Material Culture of the Peoples of Gwembe Valley,* Manchester, National Museum of Zambia, 1968.
Sykes, F. W., *With Plummer in Matabeleland,* Books of Rhod., 1972.
Ranger, T. O., *Revolt in S.R. 1896-7,* Heineman, London.
Wills, W. A. and Collinbridge, *The Downfall of Lobengula,* Books of Rhod., 1971.
Tracey, Hugh, Ngoma, Longmans, Green and Co., Cape Town.
Tracey, Andrew, *How to play the Mbira dzaVadzimu,* International Library of African Music, 1970.
Palgrave, Drummond and Coates, *Common Trees of the Highveld,* Longman, 1973, Harare.
Summers and Pagden, *The Warrior,* Books of Africa, Cape Town, 1970.
Randles, W. G. L., *The Empire of Monomotapa,* Mambo Press, Harare, 1981.
Costa, da Nogueira, *O Caso do Muenemutapa,* DH UEM, Cadernos Tempo, Maputo, 1982.
Departamento de História, UEM, Maputo, *Histó*ria de Moçambique Vol. I, 1982.